Cake Decorating for Beginners 2021

A Step-by-Step Guide to Decorating Like a Pro

Copyright © 2021

No part of this publication may be reproduced, stored in a retrieval system, or transmitted in any form or by any means, electronic, mechanical, photocopying, recording, scanning, or otherwise.

Limit of Liability/Disclaimer of Warranty: The Publisher and the author make no representations or warranties with respect to the accuracy or completeness of the contents of this work and specifically disclaim all warranties, including without limitation warranties of fitness for a particular purpose. No warranty may be created or extended by sales or promotional materials. The advice and strategies contained herein may not be suitable for every situation. This work is sold with the understanding that the Publisher is not engaged in rendering medical, legal, or other professional advice or services. If professional assistance is required, the services of a competent professional person should be sought. Neither the Publisher nor the author shall be liable for damages arising herefrom. The fact that an individual, organization, or website is referred to in this work as a citation and/or potential source of further information doesnot mean that the author or the Publisher endorses the information the individual, organization, or website may provide or recommendations they/it may make. Further, readers should be aware that websites listed in this work may have changed or disappeared between when this work was written and when it is read.

Contents

Introduction

CHAPTER ONE: Getting Ready

CHAPTER TWO: Cake Prep Basics
Basic Vanilla Cake

Double Chocolate Cake

CHAPTER THREE: Frosting Basics
Vanilla American Buttercream

Crusting Cream Cheese Frosting

Whipped Cream Frosting

Naked Cake with Fresh Fruit

Heart & Sprinkles Cake

Night Sky Ombré Cake

CHAPTER FOUR: Piping Basics
Wreath Cake

Elegant Chocolate Sheet Cake

A Little Llama Cake

CHAPTER FIVE: Fondant Basics
Homemade Marshmallow Fondant

Shades of Blue Hexagon Cake

Sweet Flowers Wedding Cake

CHAPTER SIX: Chocolate Basics
Chocolate Ganache Sweetheart

Chocolate Cake

Bright & Happy Sprinkles Cake

Measurement Conversions

Resources

Introduction

Hey there, sweet friends!

Let me start by telling you my cake story and why I wanted to write this book. Cake has been part of my dreams for almost as long as I can remember. When I was 12 years old, I asked for a cake-decorating kit for Christmas, and thankfully my parents did not disappoint. From that Christmas forward, I dreamed of growing up to own a bakery and decorate cakes. I used that set every chance I got, but for years my cake-decorating opportunities were few and far between (and pitiful, I might add).

Even as a teenager and into my twenties, I continued to do the occasional cake for church events and family members, but I was never very good at it. In the meantime, I got married. My husband and I started a family, and I graduated from college with a degree in mathematics. My main job at that time was being a stay-at-home mommy, but somewhere deep inside, I never completely lost my desire to decorate cakes.

Then, in 2009, my baby brother Jake got engaged, and for reasons I'll never understand, he asked me to make his wedding cake. Initially I said no, but when he kept asking, I decided to take the risk (or maybe *he* was the one really taking a risk), learn what I needed to learn, and go for it! That's the year *Rose Bakes* was born.

When Jake asked me to make his wedding cake, I had no idea how to make a professional cake, and I only had seven months to figure it out. I had to research, practice, and research some more to learn everything I needed to know to bake, stack, and decorate a cake that he and I could both be proud of. With almost no *real* experience of my own, I was incredibly frustrated to find that there was no single resource that provided all the information I needed.

To get some practice under my belt, I started volunteering to bake cakes for friends, family, and anyone else who would let me. After sharing a few pictures on social media, I even began to take orders before the wedding date came around. With every cake I made, I learned something new and got even more excited about seeing my dreams come true. I truly felt like I was finally doing what I was *meant* to do and using a gift God had given me.

That's when and why I started writing about cake on my blog—and why I wanted to write this book for you, the beginner cake decorator. As I learned new things, I wanted to share them with my readers. When my blog began to grow, I realized there were a lot of new cake decorators out there like myself, searching for information on how to learn the most basic of cake-decorating skills. That's when I knew I'd found my sweet spot—doing something I was passionate about and helping others do the same.

My goal is to give you, a beginner, everything you need to know to learn the art of cake decorating. From choosing the right equipment to baking delicious cakes and making them beautiful, I've tried to cover every detail. Within these pages, you'll find hundreds of photos and simple, easy-to-follow steps that will help you become a successful, confident cake decorator.

This book starts with basic cake prep—including delicious, reliable foundation recipes—and goes on to teach you how to frost and fill cakes, how to stack cake tiers, and finally how to decorate those cakes with ease. I've included troubleshooting tips for the most common problems first-time decorators are likely to run into and charts to help you mix just the right colors and know exactly how much batter you'll need.

To keep things flowing, each chapter builds on the last so that you can work your way through the book, mastering new skills and eventually combining them in ways that make the most of your creativity.

In addition to the foundational techniques, I'm sharing ten unique cakes that you'll be able to complete on your own—cakesthat will work for birthdays, baby showers, and even weddings.
The tutorials include step-by-step photos and detailedinstructions that will guide you from start to finish.

Whether you want to learn about cake decorating to make your child's dream birthday cake or you aspire to start your veryown cake business, my hope is that by the end of this book, you'llhave a solid understanding of cake decorating that will allow you to impress your kids, your friends, your family, and hopefully some clients. You may even surprise yourself!

Wishing you all the sweetest of days.

Happy Caking!

CHAPTER ONE
Getting Ready

I know how exciting it is to try something new, and I know it's tempting to just jump right in. But before you start mixing up batter, it's important to make sure you're fully prepared. In this first chapter, we'll cover all the basics you'll need to be a successful cake decorator and to tackle the instructional cakes in this book. We're going to talk about tools and equipment, food coloring, and some specialty items that will make your cake life easier.

Equipment and Tools

Some of these items are essential—these are the tools I use on almost every single cake I make. Other items are handy but not absolutely necessary. Where I can, I'll share with you my recommended tools, as well as things you might already have that will also do the job. Many of the things on this list are common household or kitchen items, while others you'll need to pick up in the cake-decorating aisle of your big-box store, at your local craft store, or online.

The good news is that you do not have to buy everything at once. You can collect and accumulate tools and equipment as you gain experience and skills. There will always be new things you can buy, but I recommend that you focus on sharpening your skills with what you have, rather than having all the latest and greatest equipment.

1. Cake pans
2. Cake turntable
3. Cake tester
4. Cooling racks
5. Cake leveler
6. Electric mixer
7. Mixing bowls
8. Measuring cups
9. Cardboard rounds
10. Offset spatulas
11. Bench scraper
12. Pattern-free paper towels
13. Pastry bags

14. Decorating tips and couplers
15. Silicone or rubber spatulas
16. Fondant smoothers
17. Rolling pins
18. Bag clips or ties
19. Scalpels and/or small, sharp paring knife
20. Bubble-tea straws
21. Dowel rods
22. Scissors
23. Cake lifter
24. Cookie cutters
25. Digital scale
26. Candy thermometer
27. Heating cores
28. Cake combs
29. Pastry wheel or pizza cutter
30. Food-safe gloves

MUST-HAVE EQUIPMENT

Cake pans: This is one of the things that you will use for years to come, and I highly recommend investing in quality, professional aluminum pans with straight sides and sharp corners. To start, a set of two or three 8-inch round pans will serve you well—this is a very common size for single-tier cakes. A 9-by-13-inch quarter-sheet pan is also a great size for most birthday sheet cakes. If you want to have a set of pans for making tiered cakes, I recommend starting with 6-inch, 8-inch, and 10-inch round pans.

Cake turntable: Without a turntable of some sort, getting a smooth finish when icing a cake will be very challenging. While a quality turntable is a hefty investment, there are alternatives that won't break the bank. You can get an inexpensive version for around $10 that will serve you well for occasional use, but you might already have other options in your kitchen. A lazy Susan is one great example. Just put it on top of a cake stand or large can of soup for more height. Another out-of-the-box option is your microwave plate if it's the kind that has the ring and wheels. Whatever your choice, using a turntable will help you get a smooth finish in no time flat (see Smooth-Frosting a Cake).

Cake tester: There are special needle-like tools available for testing the doneness of cakes. In a pinch, you can also use a skewer or toothpick.

Cake release spray: This is a spray or liquid that is a mixture of a fat (oil and/or shortening) and flour used to coat your cake pans so that cakes easily come out after baking. It's most commonly purchased as a premade spray (Baker's Joy is a widely available brand), but it can also be homemade and painted into the pans with a pastry brush.

Cooling racks: Also known as wire racks, these are necessary to properly cool a cake. Flipping your cake out of the pan onto a cooling rack allows air to circulate around all sides. If you allow a cake to completely cool inside a cake pan, there's a good chance the cake will shrink and the sides will warp. Your cake might also stick to the pan or get a soggy bottom if left to sit in the pan for too long.

Cake leveler: These come in many shapes and sizes, but for beginners I recommend an inexpensive wire leveler with a handle. If you don't have one of these, you can also use a long, serrated knife. Either tool will serve you well for leveling the tops of your cakes or for torting, or dividing, your cakes into multiple smaller layers (see [Leveling and Torting a Cake](#)).

Electric mixer: A stand mixer is preferred for making batter and frosting, but it is possible to bake and decorate cakes with a handheld mixer. This is especially true when you're just getting started and doing single or small batches. Be prepared to give your arm a workout, but it can be done!

Mixing bowls: There are no special bowls required—only that you have a few on hand in a variety of sizes (bonus points if you have bowls with matching lids that can double as storage for leftover frosting).

Measuring cups: Any standard set of wet and dry measuring cups will work. While wet and dry measuring cups technically measure the same volumes of ingredients, the design differences are related to the different things you'll be measuring. For dry cups, you can usually fill them to the brim and level off any extra with a knife to get an accurate measurement. Liquid cups usually leave more space at the top so that your ingredients don't slosh over the edge, and most of them have a spout for pouring.

Cardboard rounds: This is one thing that will not likely be in your kitchen already but is absolutely necessary when decorating cakes. You'll use them for all of your cakes, whether single- or multitiered. You will also use them for moving torted layers. I recommend having a handful for each pan size that you have, along with a few that are larger than your pans. To make your presentation nicer, I also recommend having cake paper on hand to cover your boards (see Covering a Cake Board).

Offset spatulas: Also called cake spatulas or icing spatulas, these are inexpensive and invaluable for cake decorating. I use the smaller 9-inch variety for all of my cake decorating, but some decorators prefer the larger 12-inch offset spatulas. There are also straight versions, which come in handy for larger cakes. You may want to get one of each to see which you prefer for different tasks.

Bench scraper: This tool makes achieving a flawless finish on your cake really easy. With its sharp edge held parallel to the side of your cake, you can easily achieve a smooth finish with one swipe around the sides. Bench scrapers can be purchased at hardware stores, craft stores, and in the kitchen department of some supermarkets. I recommend the 100 percent stainless steel ones that are rolled on one side (without a handle). They're usually $6 to $8 and, combined with a turntable, you will easily achieve a flawless finish on your cake (see Smooth-Frosting a Cake).

Pattern-free paper towels: Having any paper towels on hand will obviously help with the cleanup of buttery frosting and food coloring messes. Having the pattern-free kind will help you get a smooth buttercream finish (see Smooth-Frosting a Cake).

Pastry bags: Disposable bags are readily available in almost any grocery store or big-box store and make for easy cleanup. You can also purchase reusable bags, but keep in mind that they require thorough cleaning and drying after each use. I prefer disposable bags for convenience and availability, but I also always keep one or two reusable bags in my kitchen in case I happen to run low on the disposables. Large bags are the easiest to work with— I suggest no smaller than 12-inch bags, but I actually prefer 14-inch or 16-inch bags.

Decorating tips and couplers: There is an abundance of different decorating tips available and the creative possibilities are endless. For smaller tips, you will need couplers, which secure them in your pastry bags. Larger tips are also incredibly useful and don't require couplers. With a handful of basic-shaped tips, you will be able to pipe borders, flowers, stars, dots, letters, and more (see Piping 101).

Silicone or rubber spatulas: This is another tool that you may already have in your kitchen but that is extremely useful for cake decorating. Having a couple of rubber spatulas on hand makes scraping down frosting and cake batter in bowls much, much easier.

Fondant smoothers: While fondant smoothers aren't needed for buttercream cakes, these plastic tools are essential for covering a cake with fondant and getting a smooth, perfect finish.

Rolling pins: If you decorate with fondant, you will need a large rolling pin to roll it out. I also love my small rolling pin for rolling out smaller amounts of fondant for accents and details (see Working with Fondant). If investing in a good rolling pin is not possible, a length of PVC pipe is a cheap, excellent alternative. Buy the width you prefer, cut it to the desired length, clean it well, and you're good to go.

ITEMS THAT MAKE DECORATING A WHOLE LOT EASIER

Bag clips or ties: You can certainly twist the end of a pastry bag and hold it closed with your hand, but a much easier solution is to clip your bag closed after squeezing out any air. I prefer plastic bag clips, but silicone bag ties are also popular and easy to use.

Scalpels and/or a small, sharp paring knife: When working with fondant, having a small knife or scalpel is essential for cutting off excess or cutting out small shapes or letters.

Bubble-tea straws: When stacking tiers of cake, you will need some type of support in the lower tiers to support and hold the weight of the upper tiers. Otherwise, the lower tiers could possibly collapse. Bubble-tea straws are my go-to tool for stacking tiered cakes. They are lighter and easier to cut than dowel rods and support the weight of the cake very well. Havingsaid that, wood dowels are possibly a more common choice forstructuring tiered cakes. Either will work!

Dowel rods: When you have a multitiered cake, using a center dowel from top to bottom is necessary to stabilize the tiers andkeep them from moving or sliding.

Scissors: Every kitchen needs a pair of scissors, and they're extremely helpful in cake decorating. You will need them for trimming straws (like in the [Sweet Flowers Wedding Cake](#)), covering your cake boards (see [Covering a Cake Board](#)), cuttingtemplates (see [Making Figural Cakes](#)), and more.

Cake lifter: While cake boards can be used to shift or move layersof cake, having a cake lifter makes the job a little easier becauseit has a handle. You can also use a thin, flexible cutting mat for moving torted cake layers (see [Torting a Cake](#)) if you don't havea cake lifter or an extra cake board on hand.

Cookie cutters: Cutting out fondant shapes is infinitely easier when you have a cookie cutter on hand. There are thousands ofdifferent shapes and sizes available and they are generally veryaffordable.

Digital scale: Most beginners use liquid and dry measuring cupsfor measuring ingredients, which is completely acceptable. However, I've found that my measurements are more accuratewith a digital scale and I recommend using one, if possible.

Candy thermometer: In [chapter 6](#), when we start working with chocolate and ganache, having a thermometer on hand to get your chocolate to the correct temperature will take out a lot of guesswork when it comes to dripping your chocolate.

Heating cores: These are metal cones or rods with a flat nail-likehead on the bottom that help cakes bake evenly. They are especially useful for cakes larger than 10 inches in diameter, because they will radiate heat from the center of the pan to help cakes cook evenly. This will prevent the cake from having ahuge dome in the middle or the center collapsing from being undercooked.

Cake combs: While you can certainly create texture with an offset spatula or spoon (see Adding Texture to Frosting), cakecombs open the door for more defined patterns and cleaner designs.

Pastry wheel or pizza cutter: In place of a small knife, having a pastry wheel will make trimming fondant from around your cake very easy. Cutting fondant ribbons is also very easy with a wheel.If you have the kind that has a scalloped edge, you can use it tomake ruffled or decorative edges on fondant shapes.

Food-safe gloves: Cake decorating by its very nature is a messybusiness. Working with gloves keeps your hands from getting sticky and your skin from being stained with food coloring.

Food Coloring

Choosing and mixing colors into frosting or fondant are some of the most fun and satisfying parts of decorating a cake. With ninebasic colors on hand (red, orange, yellow, green, blue, purple, pink, brown, and black), the sky is the limit. There are a number of different types of food coloring available today. Let's talk about the most common and the ones recommended for cake decorating.

LIQUID COLORS

This type of coloring is the kind you'll find at your local supermarket. While it's widely available and inexpensive, it is notrecommended for cake decorating. The colors are not very intense, and you'll need a lot of it to achieve colors any brighter or deeper than pastels. Since this type of coloring is very watery, adding more of it to your frosting could potentially ruin the consistency.

GEL COLORS

This is the type of food coloring most commonly used for decorating cakes and is the most recommended. Gel colors aresold either as liquid gels in squeeze bottles or as paste gels in small jars. Because they are thicker than liquid colors, they won'tchange the consistency of frosting as easily. Gel colors are also much more concentrated—a little usually goes a long way toward achieving the color you want.

POWDER COLORS

These are more difficult to find but give you the ability to add color without adding any liquid. This is especially valuable for recipes where any extra liquid might make a significant change to the food you're creating. Another benefit to powder colors is that they cannot dry out, so they have a much longer shelf life than the other options presented here.

SPRAY COLORS

Spray colors are not used for mixing into frosting or fondant; they are applied after decorating to add color or sparkle to your cake. They come in the form of aerosol cans or in bottles to be used in an airbrush system. Unlike other colors, spray colors also come in metallics that can really transform a finished cake.

OIL-BASED COLORS

These can be used in frosting or fondant, but oil-based colors are specifically made for coloring chocolate and candy wafers. Because more common water-based colors will cause chocolate to seize, oil-based colors—sometimes called "candy colors"—are necessary.

Decorating Supplies

Cake decorating is not always about creating everything from scratch. Sometimes having sprinkles or other premade decorations can add just the right finishing touch to your cake and take it from a pretty cake to a pretty *fabulous* cake! Here are some of my favorites:

Sprinkles of all shapes, sizes, and colors: These can include jimmies, dragées, nonpareils, and more. Adding sprinkles to a cake instantly transforms it from plain to fancy.

Food-safe metallics: If it sparkles or twinkles and it's edible, it's sure to add life to your cake. This might be edible glitter, gold leaf flakes, sparkling sugars, or silver or gold stars.

Candy: What could be better than adding candy to your cake? You can use chocolates, lollipops, rock candy, peppermints, or any other candy you like to make your cake prettier and more delicious.

Cake toppers: I couldn't begin to name all the possibilities here, but these might include premade numbers or words, toys, fondant-sculpted figures, and fancy candles.

Fruit: Spring or summer cakes are especially beautiful when topped with fresh fruit to complement your flavors. Dip the fruit in chocolate or roll it in sugar, and it's even better!

Examples of cake toppers you might use on a cake include words or numbers on sticks, plastic trees, pompom picks, and fresh fruit.

Glazing Fresh Fruit for Cake Decorating

If you want to decorate your cake with fresh fruit, there's a very easy way to make it shiny and beautiful. This works for whole fruit or sliced fruit. Simply warm jelly or jam (strawberry or apple are my favorites) in the microwave with a small amount of water for 15 to 20 seconds to thin it, then brush it over the entire surface of the fruit. This glaze will make the fruit glossy and will add a little extra flavor. It will also help preserve fresh sliced fruit. A good ratio is ½ cup jam or jelly to 2 teaspoons water.

Sprinkles and candy come in every shape, size, and color. Here are rainbow nonpareils, a bright sprinkles mix, edible silver pearls, rock candy, peppermints, candy fish, tiny hearts, and gold sparkling sugar.

CHAPTER TWO

Cake Prep Basics

Now that you've got the basics under your belt, it's time to get to the good stuff: cake and frosting! We'll kick off this chapter with some recipes that will set you up for successful cake decorating. First, I'll give you a Basic Vanilla Cake recipe and a Double Chocolate Cake recipe. These are versatile recipes that you'll be able to use for layered cakes, sheet cakes, cupcakes, or carving. By the end of this chapter, you'll know how to level, stack, fill, and frost your cakes. You'll also learn several foundational techniques that you will need to understand beforeyou even pick up a piping bag.

Basic Vanilla Cake

YIELD: 9 CUPS BATTER, ENOUGH FOR 3 (8-INCH) CAKE LAYERS OR 1 (9-BY-13-INCH) SHEET CAKE
PREP TIME: 15 MINUTES   BAKE TIME: 35 TO 40 MINUTES

This from-scratch vanilla cake will be your go-to recipe for cake decorating. The flavor is perfectly delicious, and the recipe isn't at all complicated or finicky. The cake is firm enough for stacking in tiers or carving into 3-D cakes, without being too dense. It holds up beautifully under fondant while still being very moist and tender.

Just don't get distracted and overmix it! If you want a more traditional white wedding cake flavor, try adding 2 teaspoons of almond extract to the batter.

Cake release spray 1¼
cups whole milk
½ cup heavy whipping cream 2½
cups all-purpose flour
1 cup cake flour
2 teaspoons baking powder
1 cup (2 sticks) unsalted butter, at room temperature 2¾
cups sugar
1½ teaspoons salt
1½ tablespoons vanilla extract 3
large eggs

1. Preheat the oven to 325°F. Prepare three 8-inch cake pans by coating the bottoms and sides with cake release spray.

2. In a small bowl, mix together the milk and heavy cream. In a medium bowl, sift together the all-purpose and cake flours and baking powder. Set aside.

3. In a large bowl, cream the butter using an electric mixer (if you have a stand mixer, use the paddle attachment) on medium speed until it's soft and light, about 2 minutes. Add the sugar and salt and mix until the mixture is light in color and fluffy, about 2 minutes. Scrape down the sides of the

bowl often. Add the vanilla, and mix until just combined. Add the eggs, one at a time, mixing for 20 seconds after each egg, scraping down the sides of the bowl as needed.

4. Turn the mixer speed to low, then add one-third of the flour mixture and mix until just combined. Add half of the milk mixture and mix until just combined, then add another third of the flour mixture. Repeat with the remaining milk and flour mixtures. Be careful to not overmix!

5. Divide the batter between the prepared pans (approximately 3 cups of batter per pan) and spread it out evenly. Bake for 35 to 40 minutes, until a toothpick or cake tester inserted into the center of each cake comes out clean.

6. Let the cakes cool in the pans for 10 minutes, then turn out onto cooling racks to cool completely.

TIP: If you don't have a sifter or fine-mesh strainer, you can mix and fluff your dry ingredients with a whisk to get the same aerated effect as sifting.

TIP: If you don't have cake flour on hand, you can make your own with all-purpose flour and cornstarch. For each cup of cake flour, measure 1 cup all-purpose flour, remove 2 tablespoons, and add 2 tablespoons of cornstarch. Sift the mixture several times to incorporate air.

Double Chocolate Cake

YIELD: 9 CUPS BATTER, ENOUGH FOR 3 (8-INCH) CAKE LAYERS OR 1 (9-BY-13-INCH) SHEET CAKE
PREP TIME: 15 MINUTES **BAKE TIME:** 30 TO 35 MINUTES

Chocolate cake is such a classic comfort food that I had to make this one special with double the chocolate by adding mini chocolate chips. It is a dark, rich, very moist cake, yet it is sturdy enough for stacking and decorating. You can bake it as a layer cake or sheet cake and in any shape or size. I use coffee in the recipe to amp up the flavor, but you could easily substitute water and still have an amazing cake.

Cake release spray
2 cups sugar
1¼ cups all-purpose flour
1 cup cake flour
1 cup quality unsweetened cocoa powder
1 tablespoon baking soda
1½ teaspoons baking powder
1 teaspoon salt
1 cup buttermilk
1 cup cold strong brewed coffee
¾ cup vegetable oil
½ cup (4 ounces) sour cream
3 large eggs
¾ cup mini chocolate chips

1. Preheat the oven to 325°F. Prepare three 8-inch cake pans by coating the bottoms and sides with cake release spray.

2. In a large bowl, whisk together the sugar, all-purpose and cake flours, cocoa, baking soda, baking powder, and salt.

3. In a medium bowl, whisk together the buttermilk, coffee, oil, sour cream, and eggs until smooth.

4. Slowly add the buttermilk mixture to the dry mixture, using an electric mixer to beat until smooth (if using a stand mixer,

use the whisk attachment). Scrape down the sides of the bowl and gently stir in the chocolate chips.

5. Divide the batter between the prepared pans (approximately 3 cups of batter per pan) and spread it out evenly. Bake 30 to 35 minutes, until a toothpick or cake tester inserted into the center of each cake comes out clean.

6. Let the cakes cool in the pans for 10 minutes, then turn out onto cooling racks to cool completely.

For Even Baking

You want your cake layers to bake evenly to minimize the amount of trimming you might have to do. The best way to achieve this is to place your cake pans on the center rack of the oven as close to the center of the oven as possible. If you're baking multiple cake layers at once, leave at least one inch of space between the pans—never let them touch each other or the sides of the oven.

Covering a Cake Board

In the supplies list in chapter 1, I mentioned cake boards as something you must have when decorating cakes. These are necessary for presenting and moving your cakes, but a single board is usually not enough support for heavier or tiered cakes. Sometimes you need to double or triple them to provide sufficient support. Either way, when presenting a cake on a board, you should never do so on the plain corrugated cardboard. Instead, cover your board in a way that complements the cake, and your presentation will be much nicer.

NOTE: For heavy, multitiered cakes, you can buy ready-to- use cake drums, which are thicker and sturdier than cake boardsand are usually already wrapped in foil and finished.

For square or rectangular cake boards, the technique is pretty straightforward. Cut the paper approximately 3 inches wider than your board on all sides, then wrap it like a gift: foldingover the corners and then taping down all the straight edges.

For round cake boards, the process is slightly morechallenging.

Covering a Round Cake Board

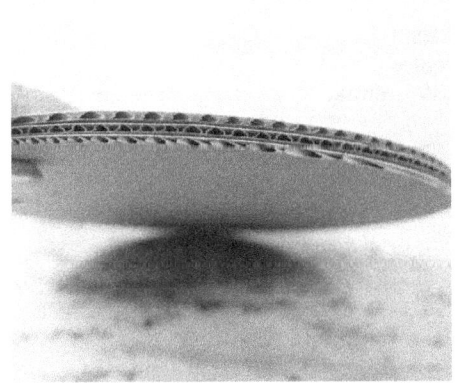

1 Use hot glue (or packing tape) to layer two or three boards together.

2 Cut foil wrap about 3 inches larger than the boards all the way around.

3 Fold the paper into pleats and tape them down every 3 to 4 inches. The finished result may not be super neat, but that's okay!

4. Using hot glue (or packing tape), attach a cake round one size smaller than the size you're covering to the bottom. This covers the messy edges and lifts the cake board slightly off your work surface, making it easier to move your cake.

5. Roll the board along your counter or work surface on all sides so that the edges are smooth. Your board is ready to use!

Make It Safe, Make It Pretty

If you finish your board with any material that is not food-safe, it's best to also add a layer of clear cellophane. While it's not necessary, I recommend wrapping the outside edge of your board with ribbon, attaching it with double-sided tape or a dot of hot glue. This adds a little extra special touch that can also complement your cake.

Leveling and Torting a Cake

While so much emphasis is put on the outside of a cake, it's also incredibly important that you give a lot of attention to the inside of the cake. In order to have a pretty cake at the end of the day, you need to have a level, smooth surface to build on. To accomplish this, you'll first learn how to level the layers of your cake, which is critical for the finished look. Leveling the cake top means cutting off the dome that naturally forms in the center of each layer when the cake is baked. There are two easy ways to do this with inexpensive tools.

You'll also learn to torte your cakes with those same tools, which means cutting a single layer into multiple thinner layers. Torting is not always necessary but can be used to add more filling and frosting on the inside, to create taller tiers, or simply because you like the dramatic look of more layers when the cake is cut.

Please note that your cake will need to be completely cooled to room temperature (not chilled) before you begin leveling or torting. If your cake is hot or warm, it may crumble. If it's cold, it will be difficult to cut through.

Leveling the Top of a Cake with a Cake Leveler

1. Place the cake on a cake board that is the same size as the cake layer. Then place the cake on a level surface.

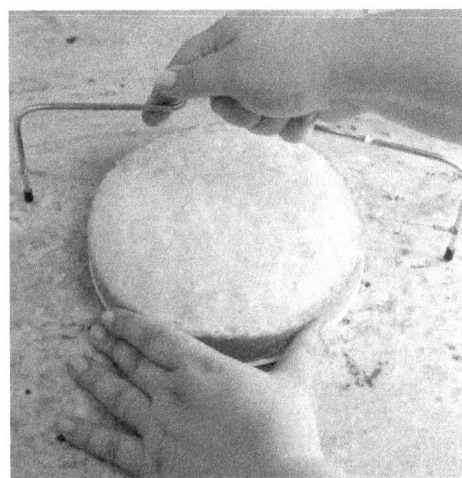

2. Adjust the wire of your cake leveler to the lowest edge of the cake dome. Holding the cake leveler by the handle, pull the cutter across the top of the cake from one side to the other.

Leveling the Top of a Cake with a Serrated Knife

1. Place the cake on a cake board that is the same size as the cake layer. Then place the cake on a turntable.

2 Place the knife at the edge of the dome on the cake and make sure it's parallel with your countertop. Keeping your elbow tight against your side to keep the knife level, rotate the turntable, sawing back and forth, until you've cut all the way through to the other side of the cake.

Torting a Cake

You can use a serrated knife or cake leveler to torte your cake layers.

1 Place the leveled cake layer on a board that is the same size as the cake, with the leveled side down.

2 Adjust the wire of your cake leveler to the desired height, making sure it is level and locked into the notches.

3 Place the cake on a flat, level surface and pull the wire of the cake leveler evenly through the cake.

4 Using a cake lifter or cake board, lift off the torted layer. Repeat for all layers.

Common Cake Fails

When baking and prepping your cakes, there are a few common problems/mistakes that come up repeatedly. Keep these tips in mind to avoid a cake disaster!

- **Cake collapses in the center.** If your cake caves in the middle, the likely problem is that you underbaked it or checked on it too soon. Always bake your cake to within five minutes of the estimated baking time before testing it for doneness. Opening the oven too soon can cause the center to collapse. When it is the correct time, use a toothpick or cake tester to verify that the cake is done before taking it out of the oven.

- **Cake sticks to the pan.** There are many techniques for preparing a cake pan, but I exclusively use cake release spray for my cakes and never have an issue. Spray your pan generously, covering the bottom, sides, and every corner and crevice. However, don't spray it on so thick that your pan is "wet"— this can lead to the bottom and sides being soggy instead of crusty.

- **Cake tears or breaks when leveling, torting, carving, or moving.** Likely your cake was not completely cool when you tried to move, level, or torte it. It takes a lot of patience to let a cake completely cool when you're excited about decorating, but this step is vital! You also shouldn't attempt to carve a warm cake for a figural cake. In fact, it's best for your cake to be chilled before carving to minimize the crumbs.

Making Figural Cakes

Years ago, specialty pans were all the rage, and there was a pan for every shape, character, and occasion. Those were fun, but they were expensive, they took up a lot of space, and many times they ended up being used only once or twice.

There's really no need to buy a specially shaped pan for most cakes. If you have a sheet pan or two (they come in a few different sizes), you can easily cut countless shapes or designs from a rectangular or square cake using a template or drawing.

The easiest way to do this is to print out the shape you want to use, cut it out, then use it as a guide on your baked and chilled cake. Cut out the shape using a very sharp knife. The biggest challenge is getting the shape or image you need printed large enough. If you have a program like PowerPoint or Excel, you can enlarge the image enough to print on multiple sheets that can be cut and taped together. If that's not an option, you can also get your local office supplies store or print shop to enlarge the image for you and print it out.

Cutting Pieces from a Sheet Cake for a Figural Cake

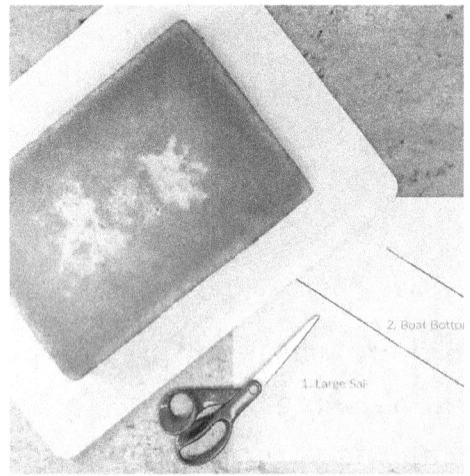

1 Bake, cool, and chill a sheet cake. Print the template you want to use for carving your cake.

2 Lay the template on the cake, marking where to make the cuts. Or use toothpicks to mark where to cut for more complicated designs.

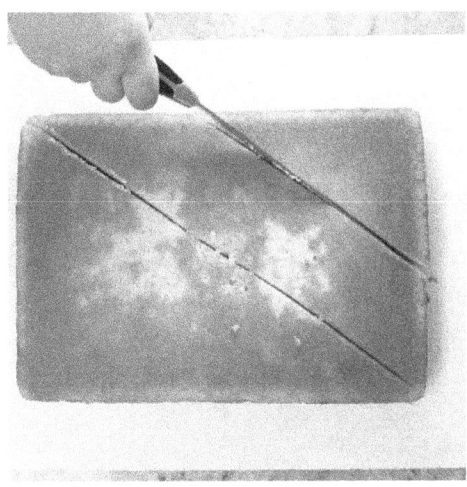

3 Cut the cake into pieces as indicated by the template.

4 Arrange the pieces into the new shape, adding frosting to help the pieces stay put, if needed.

5 Decorate!

CHAPTER THREE

Frosting Basics

Frosting is, literally and figuratively, the sweetest part of cake decorating. With some great recipes in your back pocket, you will be ready to make your cakes delicious and beautiful. I'll start you out with my go-to frosting recipes and then show you how to add color to them. Filling and frosting a cake so that it has a perfectly smooth coat is a snap with my easy-to-follow directions. I'll also teach you how to add texture in different ways for added interest. Finally, I'll take you step-by-step through the process of putting together three very different cakes that make use of the techniques in this chapter: Naked Cake with Fresh Fruit, Heart & Sprinkles Cake, and Night Sky Ombré Cake.

Frostings for Decoration

Buttercream is probably the most popular choice for cake decorating, and you'll learn here how to make Vanilla AmericanButtercream. With no cooking or whipping egg whites involved, American buttercream is blissfully simple.

You might question my inclusion of shortening, but the truth is that shortening is your best friend if you're making a cake thatneeds to hold up in a hot or humid environment. With its higher melting point, your frosting is a lot less likely to wilt or melt.
Butter gives you amazing flavor, but shortening gives you astable, more reliable frosting.

In addition to American buttercream, other frostings that areboth delicious and popular for cake decoration are cream cheese frosting and whipped cream frosting. Recipes for both are included in this chapter (see here and here, respectively).

These frosting recipes can be made with either an electric stand mixer or a heavy-duty handheld mixer. Handheld mixersare not as powerful, so mixing to the proper consistency might take longer but the results will be the same.

Vanilla American Buttercream

YIELD: 6 CUPS, ENOUGH TO GENEROUSLY FILL AND FROST A 3-LAYER (8-INCH) ROUNDCAKE OR 24 CUPCAKES
PREP TIME: 10 MINUTES

This recipe will be the foundation for most of your cake-decorating adventures in this book. The inclusion of shortening makes it stableenough to stand up to warm environments and stiff enough for piping. (If temperature and humidity are not issues, you can absolutely make an all-butter buttercream—omit the shortening anddouble the butter.)

With a few extra drops of milk, this buttercream can also be the perfect consistency for writing words on cakes and creating other intricate details. Do not overmix this frosting: Mix for no more than 3 to 5 minutes to avoid incorporating air bubbles or your frosting becoming grainy. It will be impossible to get a smooth finish on your cake if this happens. This is a very forgiving recipe: If you need it thinner, add more milk; if you need it stiffer, add more powdered sugar. It can be made in advance and will keep for two weeks in the refrigerator or up to four weeks in the freezer (simply thaw in the fridge overnight when ready to use). Most importantly, this buttercream is easy to tint with almost any type of food coloring (see[here](here)), so the sky is the limit when using it for decorating.

My clients always rave about how good my buttercream smellsand tastes—butter vanilla emulsion is the secret to that special flavor and scent.

1 cup (2 sticks) unsalted butter, at room temperature 1 cup vegetable shortening
1½ teaspoons pure vanilla extract
1½ teaspoons butter vanilla emulsion (optional)3 to 4 tablespoons milk or water, divided
¼ teaspoon salt
2 pounds (approximately 8 cups) powdered sugar

1. In a large bowl, using an electric mixer on medium speed (if

you have a stand mixer, use the paddle attachment), beat together the butter, shortening, and extracts until smooth and creamy.

2. Add 2 tablespoons of the milk or water, the salt, and half the powdered sugar and mix just until combined. Scrape down the sides of the bowl.

3. On low speed, gradually add in the remaining sugar. Add more milk or water as needed to achieve the desired consistency. If using within 2 hours, the frosting can be left at room temperature. You'll just need to keep the frosting covered with a damp cloth to prevent it from crusting. If not using within 2 hours, store the frosting in the refrigerator in an airtight container. When ready to use, bring the frosting to room temperature and rewhip it on low speed to soften before using.

VARIATION: PURE WHITE FROSTING

If you need frosting that will be stable in a hot or humid environment or if you have a bride who insists on bright white frosting with no yellow tint, omit the butter from this recipe and use 2 cups of vegetable shortening. Also, replace the pure vanilla extract with clear vanilla extract.

VARIATION: CHOCOLATE BUTTERCREAM

Add 1½ cups high-quality unsweetened natural cocoa powder and an additional 3 to 4 tablespoons of water.

FLAVOR TIP: This can serve as the base for so many other flavors. You only have to substitute some of the liquid or extracts to change the flavor to coffee, orange, rum, or coconut. You could also fold in ½ cup of lemon curd or caramel sauce.

Crusting Cream Cheese Frosting

YIELD: 6 CUPS, ENOUGH TO GENEROUSLY FILL AND FROST A 3-LAYER(8-INCH) ROUNDCAKE OR 24 CUPCAKES

PREP TIME: 10 MINUTES

Frostings made with cream cheese are either incredibly delicious buttoo soft for decorating cakes or perfect for decorating but with a barely noticeable cream cheese flavor. This recipe strikes the perfectbalance and it crusts, allowing you to smooth it to a beautiful finish.

To be certain that your frosting doesn't end up with chunks of unbeaten cream cheese, it is vital that the cream cheese be very softbefore mixing it with the other ingredients.

1 cup (2 sticks) unsalted butter, at room temperature
½ cup vegetable shortening
1 (8-ounce) package full-fat cream cheese, at room temperature1 tablespoon pure vanilla extract
¼ teaspoon salt
2½ pounds (approximately 10 cups) powdered sugar1 to 3 tablespoons milk

1. In a large bowl, using an electric mixer on low speed (if youhave a stand mixer, use the paddle attachment), beat together the butter, shortening, cream cheese, and vanillauntil completely smooth.

2. Add the salt, then gradually add the powdered sugar until combined. It will be very stiff.

3. Begin adding the milk, 1 tablespoon at a time, until you reachthe desired consistency for decorating—similar to that of peanut butter or a little thicker. Keep the frosting covered with a damp cloth until ready to use to prevent it from crusting. If you're not using it within 2 hours, store in the refrigerator in an airtight container. When ready to use, bringto room temperature and rewhip it on low speed to soften.

Whipped Cream Frosting

YIELD: 4 CUPS, ENOUGH TO FILL AND FROST A 3-LAYER (8-INCH) ROUND CAKE OR 18 CUPCAKES
PREP TIME: 10 MINUTES

Whipped cream frosting is a lighter, not-so-sweet alternative to buttercream. But sadly, it holds its shape for only a very short while and then begins to deflate. By adding powdered milk, the frosting is stabilized so that it can be piped and used similarly to buttercream.

Whipped cream frosting does not have enough substance to pipe a dam or use as a thick layer of filling, but it can be spread thin between layers of cake. It will also hold its own for piped decorations and will last long enough to make a day or two ahead without fear of it melting or losing its shape.

2½ cups very cold heavy whipping cream
1 cup powdered sugar
2 tablespoons nonfat powdered milk
1½ teaspoons pure vanilla extract

1. In a large bowl, using an electric mixer on low speed, beat the cream, powdered sugar, milk, and vanilla together just until combined.

2. Scrape down the sides of the bowl, then mix on high speed just until the frosting thickens and stiff peaks form. If you can swipe a spoon through the frosting and the frosting doesn't fall back into the space, it's ready.

VARIATION: CHOCOLATE WHIPPED CREAM FROSTING

Sift 5 tablespoons unsweetened natural cocoa powder into the powdered sugar before adding to the bowl.

TIP: Using a chilled bowl and/or whisks will help the frosting whip up to stiff peaks more quickly. Also, do not walk away while making this frosting. Overmixing will cause your whipped cream to separate and turn into butter! If this happens, it cannot be fixed. You must start over.

Thick or Thin (or Somewhere in Between)?

The consistency of your buttercream frosting is a really important factor in how successful you will be at decorating a cake with it. If it's too thin, borders and flowers will not hold their shape. If it's too thick, it will be hard to squeeze out of the bag and lines or fine details will break or crack.

Getting the perfect consistency does not come with hard-and-fast rules. Everything from the temperature and humidity in your kitchen to the brands of your ingredients can play a factor in the texture of your buttercream. However, there are some general guidelines you can use to correct any issues. If your frosting is too stiff, add milk (a few drops at a time) to thin it to the desired consistency. If it's too thin, add small amounts of powdered sugar as needed to stiffen it up.

Thinner frosting is needed for writing letters and piping fine lines or details. A medium consistency is needed for most applications—including covering your cake and piping borders, flowers, and ruffles. Stiff frosting is not often used but is especially helpful for piping dams when filling and stacking your cake layers (see Filling a Cake Using a Dam).

Approximate amounts of frosting needed to fill and frost 3-layer cakes (approximately 5 inches tall)

ROUND PANS	6-inch	4 cups
	8-inch	5 cups
	10-inch	6 cups
	12-inch	7 cups
SQUARE PANS	6-inch	4½ cups
	8-inch	5½ cups
	10-inch	7 cups
	12-inch	8½ cups

Adding Color to Frosting

Coloring frosting is easy and so much fun. Deciding on the right color or colors can set the mood for your cake and bring it to lifelike nothing else. Keep in mind that coloring frosting is not an exact science, so you may have to experiment with mixing and combining colors to find just the right shade for your project. I recommend keeping a set of primary and secondary colors on hand at all times. The nine basic colors you should have are red, orange, yellow, green, blue, purple, pink, brown, and black. With these, you can mix and match almost any color you desire.

Achieving these basic colors is somewhat intuitive and will get easier with practice. If you're going for a pastel or light color, it's best to add coloring in small increments with a toothpick or other small tool. If your end goal is a deep or rich color, you can add it in larger quantities by squeezing in big drops or using a knife to add a larger amount. Either way, add your coloring incrementally and be patient. To avoid adding more air to your frosting, it's best to fold or stir color into the frosting using a large spoon or silicone spatula.

After adding the coloring, if you let the frosting rest for a short time, you'll know if you need to add more color or if you've gotten the shade you want. It's best to make dark or rich colors at least a couple of hours ahead of time so that the colors have an opportunity to develop (see [Getting Deep Colors](#)).

For [Vanilla American Buttercream](#) and [Crusting Cream Cheese Frosting](#), stirring the color into the finished frosting is easy, and you can continue to add color as needed until you get the desired shade.

For [Whipped Cream Frosting](#), it's best to add the color to the liquid *before* whipping. Adding color after whipping can destabilize the frosting and ruin the texture. For this reason, it's more difficult to gauge the final color that you'll end up with, and you cannot add more color after the cream mixture is whipped.

CUSTOM COLORS

COLOR	FOOD COLORING MIX
Egg yolk	5 parts yellow/1 part orange
Coral	3 parts yellow/1 part red
Watermelon	3 parts pink/1 part red
Fuchsia	5 parts pink/1 park purple
Maroon	5 parts red/1 part green
Slate blue	4 parts blue/1 part black
Teal	4 parts blue/1 part yellow
Lime green	9 parts yellow/1 part green
Forest green	5 parts green/1 part black
Gray	1 part black

Getting Deep Colors

When coloring buttercream, it's important to note that deep or rich colors always take more time to develop. It's recommended that you mix them at least a couple of hours ahead of time or the night before, if possible. The most troublesome colors are black, deep or rich red, and dark blues and greens. Here are some tips for those hard-to- achieve colors:

Black: As long as there's no objection to chocolate, adding cocoa powder to your buttercream before adding black coloring will give you a nice start on achieving the darkest black. Once you have a dark brown frosting, begin adding the black gel coloring and mixing until you get a deep, dark shade of charcoal gray. You might also have to add additional drops of water or milk if the cocoa powder makes your butter-cream too stiff. Let the buttercream rest for an hour or more for you to see the black develop, then add more black gel if needed.

Bright or deep red: To get a bright red, start by making a dark shade of pink. Then add red gel coloring a few drops at a time until you get close to the desired color. Again, let the buttercream rest for an hour or more to see if it develops into the red you want. For a deeper red, add a tiny drop of brown or black gel coloring.

Dark green, blue, or purple: Use leaf green, royal blue or navy blue, and regal purple to get a good foundation for the blue, green, or purple shade you want. After getting a color close to the depth you want, add a tiny drop of brown or black to deepen the color to a more dramatic hue.

Adding Color to Buttercream

1 Add small amounts of color to the prepared buttercream using a toothpick or other small tool.

2 Gently fold or stir the color into the buttercream.

3 Continue to stir until the coloring is fully mixed in. Add another drop or two if you want a darker shade and mix that in the same way.

Filling and Stacking Cake Layers

After leveling and torting your cake layers (see <u>here</u>), you still have two more steps before you get to the fun part of decorating: You need to fill and stack the cake. There are many ways to do this, but you are going to learn my favorite way: the way that yields a lot of yummy frosting and/or filling inside.

To keep all that filling from bulging out on the sides of your cake, you will need to create a dam of frosting that holds it in.

This is especially important if your filling is different from your frosting or if you plan to add any other flavors to the inside (such as a fruit spread or cookie crumbles).

Filling a Cake Using a Dam

For this technique, you will need to fill a piping bag halfway with a stiff-consistency frosting and use a large round opening (approximately ½ inch in diameter). You could also use a coupler without the coupler ring or a piping tip.

1 Place one layer of cake, leveled-side down, onto a cake round and pipe a dam of frosting around the top edge of the cake.

2 Fill inside the dam with a medium-consistency frosting or the filling of your choice. If using buttercream, fill until level with the top of the dam. If using preserves or another soft filling, fill until slightly below the height of the frosting dam. If you're using a soft filling that you do not want to seep into the cake, add a thin layer of frosting before adding the filling.

3 Stack the next layer of cake on top. Make sure it is level and even on all sides with the layer of cake beneath it. Slightly press down to remove any air, then pipe a dam on top of it and fill in the same way.

4 Repeat these steps for all layers except the last. Place the last layer on top, cut-side down, making sure it is also level and even on all sides.

The Perfectly Frosted Cake

Nothing is more disappointing than getting crumbs in your frosting, which makes everything look messy. Crumb-coating your cake means applying a thin layer of frosting to catch all of the crumbs and seal them in before applying your final layer of frosting. Once your cake is crumb coated, it needs to be chilled for about 15 minutes. Then you can add a thicker layer of fresh frosting for a smooth finish.

Buttercream is dense and heavy, so in addition to sealing in the crumbs, crumb-coating gives your final layer of frosting and any applied decorations something to adhere to. This prevents disasters like borders falling off or layers of buttercream bubbling up and pulling away from the cake.

Some cake decorators skip the step of crumb-coating. It takes serious skills to frost a cake without pulling away any crumbs or having your spatula scrape against the cake. This is not recommended for beginners.

Crumb-Coating a Cake

1 With your cake on a turntable, place a large scoop of thinner-consistency frosting in the center of the top cake layer. Using a small angled spatula, spread it out to the edges. This layer may be thin enough to see through, but it needs to be thick enough to catch all of the crumbs. Do your best to not allow your spatula to come into direct contact with the cake.

2 Push any excess frosting from the top edge down onto the sides of the cake. Add more frosting as needed to completely cover the sides. Turn the cake on the turntable and continue adding frosting and smoothing as needed until it's covered on all sides.

3 Swipe away any excess frosting on the sides and on the top of the cake to finish the crumb coat. This thin layer of frosting does not need to be perfect. You only need to be sure that you have entirely covered the cake to seal in the crumbs and have a fairly smooth surface for your final layer of frosting. Chill the cake for at least 15 minutes before frosting.

Smooth-Frosting a Cake

For this, you will need a small angled spatula, a bench scraper, a texture-free paper towel (Viva® is the best brand for this), and a fondant smoother.

1. With the crumb-coated cake on a turntable, place a large amount of medium-consistency frosting in the center.

2. Spread it toward the edges. Rotate as you spread for an even layer about ¼ inch thick.

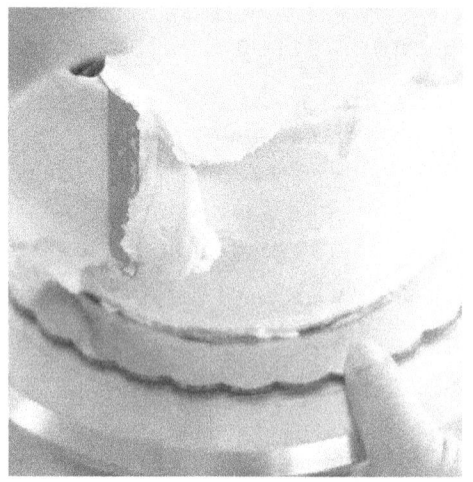

3 Working in small sections, add dollops of frosting to the sides of the cake and completely cover the crumb coat with a layer of frosting about ⅓ inch thick.

4 Holding a bench scraper slightly pressed into the frosting, rotate all the way around to get a smooth finish. This will create a lip of frosting on top. Clean the scraper.

5 Place the bench scraper at the top edge of the cake just outside the lip of frosting and hold it at a 45-degree angle. Begin pulling the lip of frosting inward toward the center of cake, smoothing it and lifting off any excess. This motion will create a sharp edge on the cake while removing the extra frosting. Wipe that excess back into your bowl after each swipe. Continue this process until the top of the cake is even and smooth.

6 You can stop at step 5, but for a flawless finish, allow the frosting to dry or "crust" for at least 15 minutes. Then gently hold the paper towel to the side of the cake and lightly run a fondant smoother over it to smooth the surface. Rotate the turntable, moving the paper towel after each section is smoothed, until you've completed the sides.

7 Repeat step 6 on the top of the cake.

How to Use a Cake Turntable

A cake turntable will be one of your best friends in cake decorating. Put a small non-skid mat or surface underneath your cake to keep it from sliding around, and always make sure the cake is centered on the stand. To get a smooth finish, the best combination of tools is a bench scraper and a great turntable. Here is the best way to get that perfect turn.

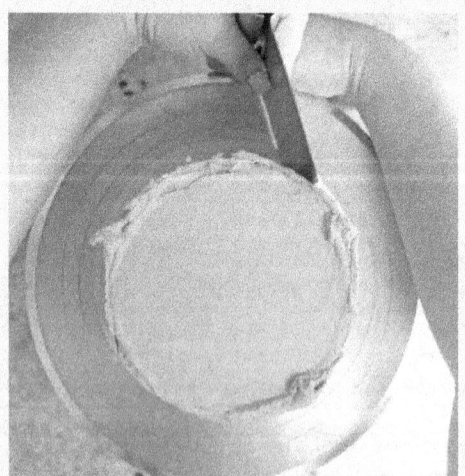

1 Reach your dominant hand around to the back of the turntable at approximately a 12 o'clock position. With your other hand, place the bench scraper on the cake with the edge slightly pressed into the frosting, also at the 12o'clock position.

2 Begin rotating the turntable clockwise while pulling the bench scraper toward you counterclockwise with your other hand. Continue to rotate until your hands meet at your starting point on the front side of the cake stand. This will give you a perfectly smooth finish with none of the marks made by rotating a stationary cake plate multiple times.

Adding Texture to Frosting

While a flawless, perfectly smooth cake is something every cake decorator wants and needs to know how to achieve, there are several rustic or rough-finished techniques that are incredibly popular and don't require the perfection of smoothing. These can be achieved with something as simple as a spoon from yourkitchen or an inexpensive cake comb.

Using a Spoon or Small Offset Spatula to Create Swirls

With a medium-consistency frosting, use a spoon to add dollops of frosting to a crumb-coated cake. You can swirl it around or swipe it in small motions to create waves or swooshes of frosting on the top and sides of the cake.

Using a Spoon or Small Offset Spatula to Create Lines

Starting with a smooth-finished cake on a turntable (following steps 1 through 5 of Smooth-Frosting a Cake), use the back of a spoon to create a lined texture on your cake. You will want to do this technique before the buttercream crusts. Start at the bottom, holding the spoon horizontally, and use your other hand to rotate the turntable, gradually moving up the side of the cake. Repeat this technique on the top of the cake, starting along the outside edge and working toward the center.

Using a Cake Comb

Cake combs come in many sizes, shapes, and patterns and can

be used to create a variety of classic looks. It's more difficult to see flaws with smaller patterns, so those are best for beginners. You will want to use cake combs on buttercream cakes that have not yet crusted.

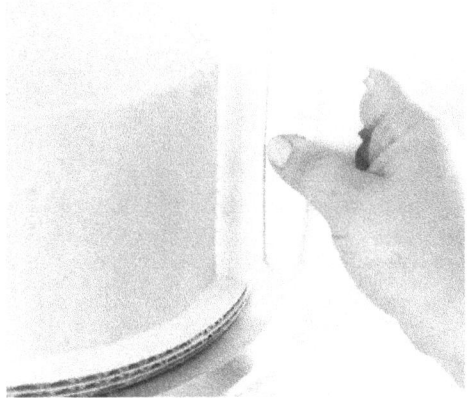

1 Starting with a smooth-finished cake on a turntable (following steps 1 through 5 of Smooth-Frosting a Cake), hold the side of the comb parallel to the side of the cake.

2 Lightly touch the surface of the frosting and begin rotating the turntable, dragging the edge of the comb through the frosting to create a lined pattern.

This cake was simply decorated with a small offset spatula to create the line texture and some fresh flowers to add a pop of color. The end result is an elegant cake perfect for almost any occasion.

INSTRUCTIONAL CAKE

NAKED CAKE with FRESH FRUIT

So-called "naked" cakes are some of the easiest to put together. By adding a simple topper like fresh fruit or edible flowers, a naked cake becomes elegant. The amount of buttercream you leave on will change the look dramatically—from a completely naked cake with no frosting on the outside to a "barely naked cake" where you can only see hints of cake peeking through. Practice is key to finding a look that you like and how much frosting to leave or scrape off. This cake is somewhere in between, which is my favorite look.

TECHNIQUES USED:

Filling and Stacking a Cake Crumb-Coating a Cake Smooth-Frosting a Cake Glazing Fresh Fruit

YOU'LL NEED:

3 (8-inch) cake layers, stacked and filled with 2 cups Vanilla American Buttercream 1 cup Vanilla American Buttercream, for decorating, as desired Finished cake board Turntable
Small spatula Bench
scraper Fresh
strawberries
Strawberry jelly or jam Small
pastry brush

1 Place your filled and chilled cake on a turntable.

2 Cover the top with frosting, then push it over the edge to cover the side with a thinlayer. Add more frosting as needed to cover the cake.

3 Run a bench scraper around the outside of the cake, removing most of the excess frosting but leaving a thin layer you can see through in places.

4 Use the spatula to scrape from the top edge toward the center and smooth away the lip of frosting. Rotate the cake until the top edge is sharp and clean.

5 Glaze the strawberries with warmed jelly or jam mixed with water.

6 Arrange the berries on the top and/or around the bottom of the cake.

INSTRUCTIONAL CAKE
HEART & SPRINKLES CAKE

This cake can be adapted for almost any celebration. You canuse a cookie cutter in the shape of a number to represent a birthday age or, instead of a heart, use a star or flower cookie cutter for different themes. With a few simple tools and somepretty sprinkles in any colors you like, the possibilities are endless. This is a vanilla cake, smooth-frosted with **Whipped Cream Frosting**, then decorated.

TECHNIQUES USED:

Filling and Stacking a CakeCrumb -Coating a Cake Smooth-Frosting a Cake

YOU'LL NEED:

3 (8-inch) cake layers, stacked, filled, crumb-coated, smooth-frosted with 4 cups Whipped Cream Frosting, and chilled Turntable
Large baking sheet
Rainbow nonpareils
Small offset spatula or small knife
Heart cookie cutter (or other number/shape of choice)Small spoon

1 Place the chilled, smooth-frosted cake on a turntable. Place the turntable on a large baking sheet.

2 Pour or scoop the sprinkles into your dominant hand. Holding the turntable with your other hand, gently press them into the side of the cake around the bottom edge. Once you have an area covered to your liking, turn the cake slightly and repeat on the next section. Continue until there are sprinkles all around the bottom of the cake.

3 Using a small offset spatula or knife, carefully wipe away any excess sprinkles from the cake board.

4 Place the cookie cutter in the center of the top of the cake.

5 Use the spoon to pour sprinkles inside the cookie cutter to cover the frosting.

6 Use the spatula to spread the sprinkles out evenly.

7 Remove the cookie cutter and gently pick off any stray sprinkles with a sharp knife.

INSTRUCTIONAL CAKE
NIGHT SKY OMBRÉ CAKE

This is the perfect dessert for your sky-loving teenager or friend who loves astronomy. The ombré design, where a single color fades from a dark to a light shade (or vice versa), is perfect for asky representation. The design is also easily adapted to different color themes or made more special by adding a gold number or other unique topper. A moon-and-stars-themed baby shower would be perfectly complete with this cake in lighter shades of blue.

TECHNIQUES USED:

Filling and Stacking a Cake Crumb-Coating a Cake Adding Color to Buttercream
Using a Spoon or Small Offset Spatula to Create Lines

YOU'LL NEED:

3 (8-inch) cake layers, stacked, filled with 3 cups Vanilla American Buttercream, crumb-coated, and chilled
3 cups Vanilla American Buttercream, for decorating, divided Royal blue gel coloringBlack gel coloring
Finished cake board
Turntable
Small cake spatulaStar
sprinkles

1. Divide the buttercream equally into 3 bowls. To the first bowl, add a small drop of royal blue coloring. To the second bowl, add 2 drops of royal blue coloring. To the last bowl, add 2 drops of royal blue coloring and 1 drop of black coloring. Mix until the color is fully incorporated in each bowl. Remember, for richer colors, allow the frosting to sit, covered with a damp paper towel, at room temperature for at least 1 to 2 hours before using.

2. Place the chilled, crumb-coated cake on a finished cake board, then place it on a turntable. Using a small spatula, cover the top and one-third of the way down the

sides of the cake with the darkest buttercream. It does not need to be perfect at this point, but you do want a significant layer of frosting.

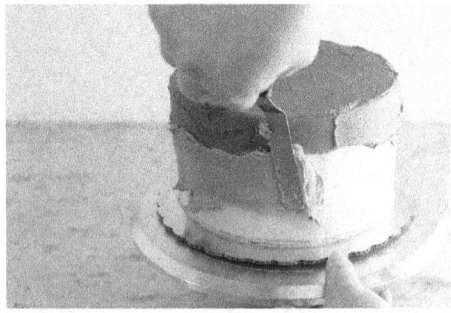

3 Below that, add the medium shade of blue frosting, spreading it in a band around the middle of the cake.

4 Do the same with the lightest blue frosting around the bottom third of the cake.

5 Using a bench scraper, gently smooth the frostings on the sides so that they blend and you get an even layer of thickness.

6 Using the spatula and rotating the turntable, create a lined texture along the side of the cake from bottom to top.

7 Create a lined texture on the top of the cake.

8 Add star sprinkles to the top and press handfuls of sprinkles along the bottom of the sides of the cake.

CHAPTER FOUR
Piping Basics

Yay! You have baked a delicious cake, filled and frosted it with buttercream, and have a beautiful, smooth canvas for your design. Now you get to dive into the art of cake decorating and piping shapes on cakes is the most classic form. From borders to words and flowers to dots, you'll learn several different types of piping that can be used on cakes for any occasion. We'll also talkabout the different kinds of pastry bags available—both reusableand disposable—as well as piping tips and couplers. Frosting consistency, the pressure you apply to the bag, and the angle that you hold it at are key to great piping work. With time and practice, you will be able to pipe stars, dots, lines, flowers, ruffes, and many other shapes.

So let's get started!

Pastry Bags

Pastry bags (also called piping bags) come in a variety of sizes; I find that bigger is usually better to prevent overflowing and messy refills. My preferred size is the 14-inch bag, but any size from 12-inch to 16-inch bags are workable sizes that can be easily manipulated, while still holding enough frosting so that you don't have to constantly refill.

Both reusable and disposable piping bags are found in craftstores and online. In my opinion, either is fine for most cake-decorating applications. However, there are a few differences that you should be aware of so that you can decide which type of bag you would like to use.

REUSABLE PASTRY BAGS

Reusable pastry bags are somewhat easier to grip, because they are made from textured fabric or canvas, not plastic. They're also more environmentally friendly and, with proper care, will last for years. I had one bag that came with the kit I got as a teenager that lasted more than 20 years before it finally came apart at the seam. If you're going to use reusable bags, it's best to invest in higher-quality fabric ones that are thin and soft and don't allow oil to seep through.

On the downside, reusable bags require more care. You have to turn them inside out and wash with very hot, soapy water to get all of the greasy residue out of them, which can be messy.
They need to be completely dry before storing, and if you use a lot of different colors of frosting, you will need to have several on hand or wash them often. Also, once the end is cut off, you're locked into the size coupler and piping tips you can use.

DISPOSABLE PASTRY BAGS

By contrast, disposable pastry bags are inexpensive and convenient. They are meant to be used only once and can be tossed at the end of each cake job. They come in large quantities and are especially handy if your cake design requires multiple colors. The same goes for the size of piping tips and couplers, because you can cut them to different sizes based on which tips you're using. Finally, disposable bags are readily available almost anywhere cake supplies are sold, including local grocery stores and big-box stores.

The biggest downside for disposable bags, other than the environmental impact, is that plastic bags are slick. They can easily slip out of your hand if you're not careful—especially if you get any frosting on your hands or the outside of the bag. For this reason, I sometimes wrap a paper towel around my bag where I'm gripping it to help me hold it more securely.

With either type of bag, if you're using standard-size piping tips, you will also need to use a coupler. This is a small, usually plastic adapter that goes into the piping bag and has a ring that screws onto the outside of the bag to hold the piping tip in place. Using a coupler allows you to easily switch out different tips without changing bags. Couplers are not needed for the large piping tips that are used for some cake and cupcake designs because they're not as easily pushed out of the bag.

Preparing and Filling a Pastry Bag

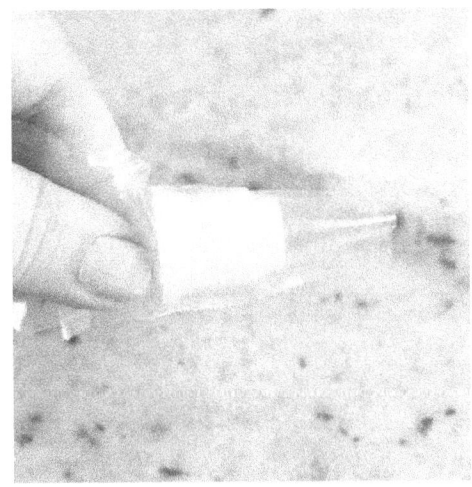

1 Cut the end off the tip of the pastry bag, no more than an inch. Remove the ring from the coupler and drop the base into the piping bag. Squeeze it down as far as it will go, narrow end first.

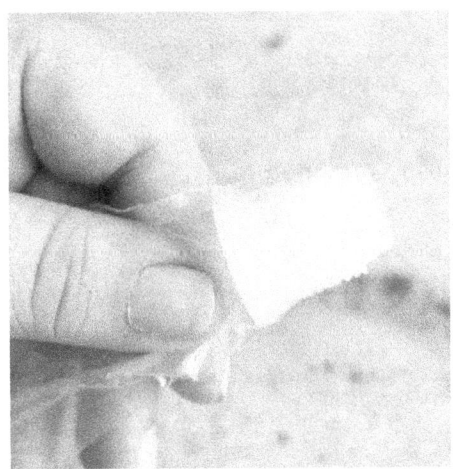

2 If needed, cut the tip again ⅛ inch at a time until the coupler sticks out of the bag no more than half its length. Be careful: If you cut too much, the coupler will pop out when you begin to squeeze the frosting.

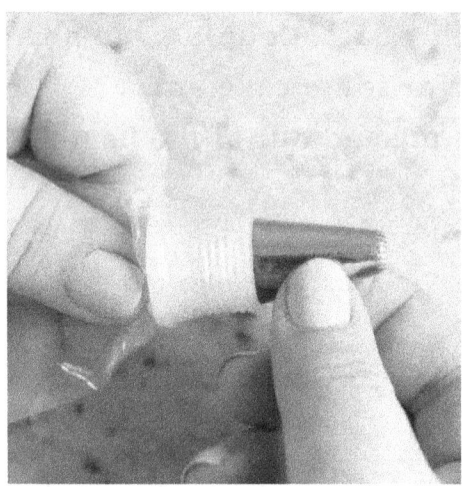

3 After the coupler base is properly inserted into the bag, place a piping tip over the base.

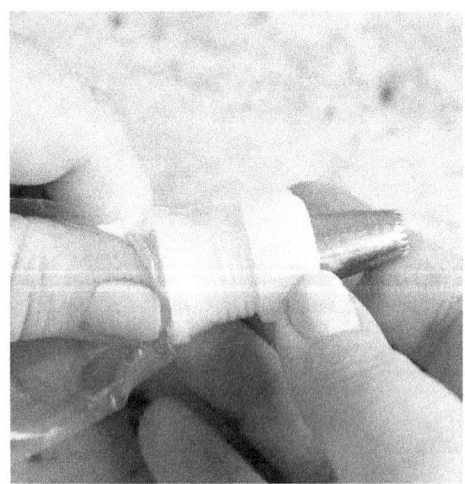

4 Place the ring over the tip and screw it onto the base, securing the tip in place.

5 To fill the bag, place it in a jar or vase (for larger bags) and fold the top of the bag out and over the edge of the glass. Open it wide.

6 Scoop the frosting into the bottom of bag using a large spoon or silicone spatula, filling no more than two-thirds full. Overfilling the bag makes it difficult to hold and could potentially lead to a mess.

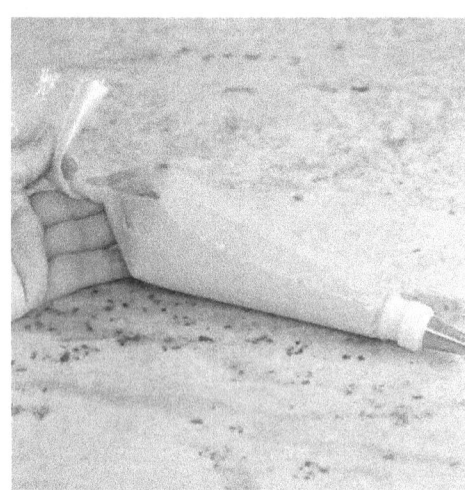

7 Twist the top of the bag tightly closed, then secure it with a bag clip or tie. If you do not have a clip or tie, hold the bag tightly twisted while you work, or frosting will besqueezed out of the back of the bag.

8 When working, always place your hand on the bag above the frosting, rather thanin the middle of the bag.

Decorating Tips

I love collecting cake-decorating tips and have an embarrassingly large stash of them. Decorating tips are usuallymetal, but you can also find plastic ones. The shape of the tip iswhat makes your buttercream decorations beautiful and uniqueand most are identified by a number on the side.

There are two common sizes of tips: standard and large. Standard-size tips are usually ¾ inch wide at the base and require a coupler. Tips larger than standard size have become increasingly more popular and are generally used without a coupler.

It's essential that you clean your tips thoroughly after each use to prevent rust or a build-up of greasy residue on the inside. They're easily cleaned by holding them under very hot water to rinse out the bulk of any buttercream, then using a brush to scrub them with more hot water and soap. Allow them to dry completely on a towel before storing or nesting them.

While the sky is the limit on the shapes, sizes, and number of tips available, there are some essential piping tips that are good for every cake decorator to have on hand. Here are the basic shapes I recommend:

ROUND TIPS

Standard round tips are used for piping lines, dots, scrollwork, tiny pearl borders, and lettering. Large round tips are perfect for piping large dot borders, clouds of frosting on cupcakes, or the stiff frosting dams used when filling a cake (see [Filling a Cake Using a Dam](#)).

STAR TIPS

Star tips are available in both open and closed designs. They each yield a slightly different look when piped, but the applications are similar. Standard-size star tips, both open and closed, are the go-to piping tip for scalloped or shell borders but are also commonly used for scrollwork, simple flowers, tiny rosettes, or a filled-in star texture on a cake. Large star tips are also used for borders, as well as for large rosettes covering a cake or a single rosette on a cupcake. Star tips also include "French tips," which have much smaller ridges and more of them, resulting in a unique look when piped.

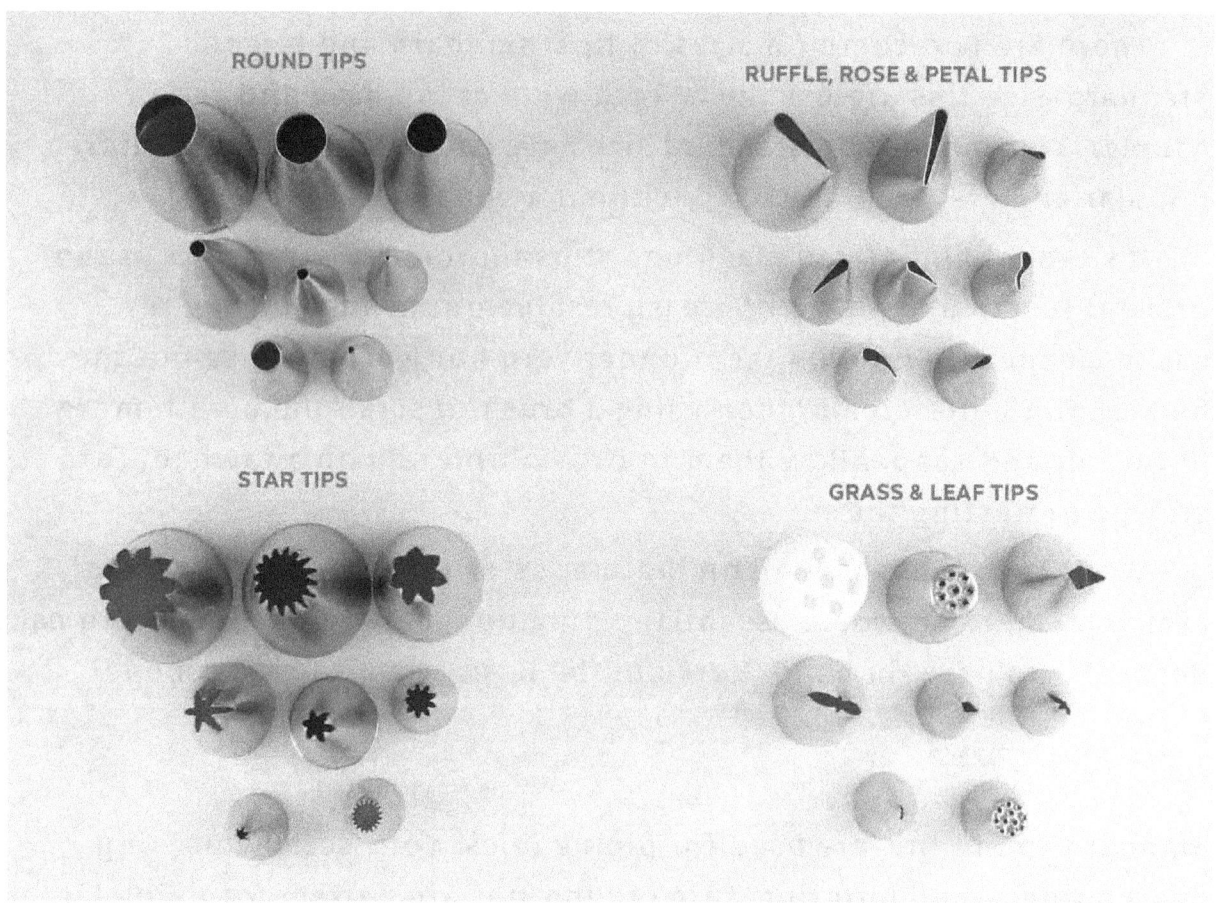

RUFFLE, ROSE, AND PETAL TIPS

Originally called petal tips because they were used to make the classic buttercream rose petals, these tips are also used for other types of flower petals and to make buttercream ruffles. The ruffles can be piped onto the sides and top of the cake for a beautiful effect. Petal tips can be straight or curved and, as with the other types of tips, come in both standard and large sizes.

GRASS AND LEAF TIPS

As the names indicate, these tips are meant for piping leaves and grass. Depending on the leaf tip chosen, many different sizes and shapes of leaves can be piped. A grass tip is also the perfect tool for piping "hair." Both the leaf and grass tips come in standard and large sizes, and which size you choose will depend on the design you are working on. You may also find grass tips sold as "multi-hole" tips.

Piping 101

Over time you will develop your own style of piping. With practice, you'll figure out what works for you and what doesn't and how you're most comfortable. However, there are some foundational principles that will get you started down the rightpath and help you find success as you learn to pipe frosting.

HOW MUCH TO FILL THE PASTRY BAG

You learned how to fill the pastry bag [here](), but let's talk a little more about that. As previously mentioned, I never recommend using pastry bags smaller than 12 inches. It's very easy to overfillthe smaller bags, and it becomes a mess when the frosting spillsout of the back end.

Additionally, I recommend never filling a bag more than two-thirds full. If you overfill any bag, it becomes heavy, difficult to hold, difficult to control, and especially difficult to keep twisted closed if you're not using a clip or tie.

If you are not covering an entire cake and therefore do not need a large amount of frosting, I recommend filling it even lessthan halfway. This is particularly true when piping small lines or letters. Fill the bag with only enough frosting so that you can hold the bag in the palm of your hand. If you do this, it will be much easier to hold the bag steady and get consistent results.

WORKING UNDER PRESSURE

To get the best results when piping, you will want to exert a steady, uniform amount of pressure on the bag. The more pressure you apply, the faster the frosting will come out of the bag, so if you don't have good control over your bag, this couldquickly turn into a decorating disaster.

Pressure can be light, moderate, or heavy. The amount of

pressure applied needs to "match" the speed at which you're piping. If you're applying light pressure, you'll want to be moving the bag very slowly and gently. For moderate pressure, you'll want to move at a medium speed, and for heavy pressure, you'll need to be working quickly to keep up with the amount of frosting coming out of the bag.

For example, if you're writing text on a cake and you struggle with good handwriting (as I do), you would likely want to use very gentle pressure and move slowly so that you don't mess it up. On the other hand, if you're piping a border that you're confident you can do well, you would exert a lot of pressure and move quickly around the edges of the cake.

How to Hold a Pastry Bag

45-DEGREE ANGLE: Holding the bag at a slant, 45 degrees from the surface of the cake, is common for piping borders or scrollwork and writing text on a cake.

90-DEGREE ANGLE: Holding the bag straight up and down, perpendicular to the surface of the cake, is common for rosettes, dots, and stars.

Practice, Practice, Practice

The biggest secret I can tell you about perfecting piping is this: *There is no secret.* You simply have to keep doing it — over and over and over again until you get it right, build confidence, and learn what works for you. There's no substitute for an excessive amount of hands-on work.

And there's no need to waste cakes in the process. For practice, you can pipe onto the back of a cookie sheet, wipe it off, and start again. Or you can pipe directly onto your countertop, if that's your best option. If you don't want to wash the counter or dishes, pipe onto sheets of parchment paper that you can toss when you're done.

The bottom line is this: Start piping and keep piping. Pipe letters and words, practicing the style of font or script you like best. Practice stars and pay attention to how much pressure you need to exert to get them all the same size—then pipe them over and over again. Make drop flowers, rosettes, or leaves again and again until they start to take shape and look like you want them to. You can even print templates to help you practice piping straight lines or certain fonts.

Frosting a Cake with a Pastry Bag

Tip #808

Position: 90-degree angle from the surface of the cake Medium-consistency frosting

If you choose to use this method to cover a cake in buttercream, you can skip crumb- coating altogether. You only need to be careful not to bump your piping tip onto the side of the cake and drag any crumbs into the frosting.

1. Place the stacked and filled cake on its final cake board and then on the cake turntable.

Starting at the bottom, hold your piping bag perpendicular to the side of the cake. With even pressure, begin piping a long rope at the bottom, next to the cakeboard, turning the turntable as you go. Many times, you can let the momentum of your piping do a lot of the work of turning the turntable at a steady pace as you pipe.

2 Once you make a complete round, keep going in the same manner with a long rope of frosting above the first. Continue in this way until you reach the top.

3 Hold the bag at a 45-degree angle at the center of the top of the cake. Begin turning the turntable and pipe a rope of buttercream in a spiral until the top of the cake is covered.

4 Continue until the edge of the cake is reached and the entire cake is covered.

Note: At this point, you can leave the cake as is with a spiral design or follow steps 4 to 6 of Smooth-Frosting a Cake.

Piping Stars and Dots

Tip #4 (dot) and #17 (star)

Position: 90-degree angle from the surface of the cake

Medium-consistency frosting

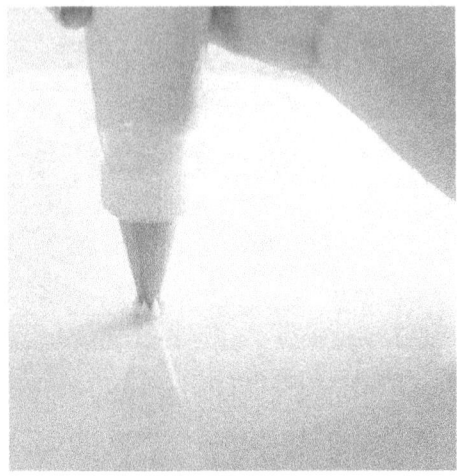

1 Start by holding the piping bag straight up, slightly above the surface of the cake.

2 Squeeze the bag with moderate pressure. The heavier the pressure, the larger the star or dot will be.

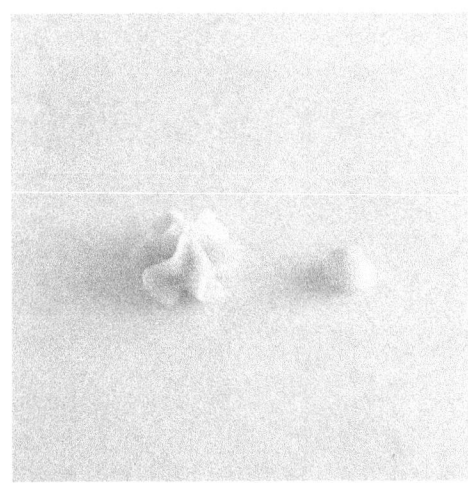

3 Releasing all pressure, lift the tip straight up and away from the cake to finish the shape.

Piping Swirl Flowers

Tip #16

Position: 90-degree angle from the surface of the cake

Medium-consistency frosting

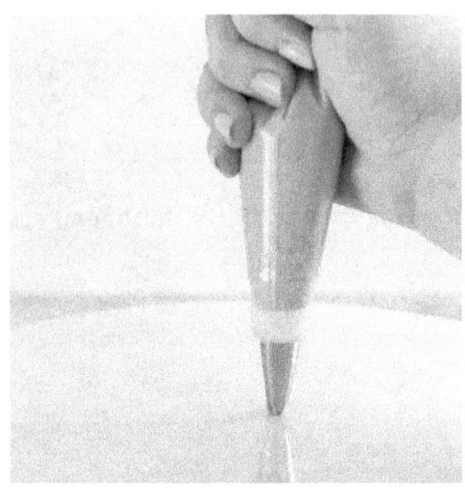

1 Start by holding the piping bag straight up, slightly above the surface of the cake, and begin piping a star.

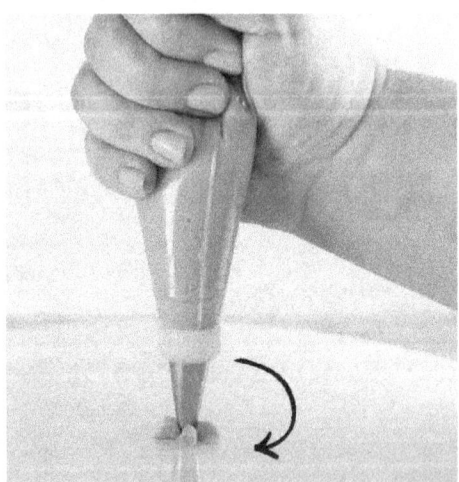

2 While you apply pressure, begin twisting your wrist until you make a full rotation toward yourself.

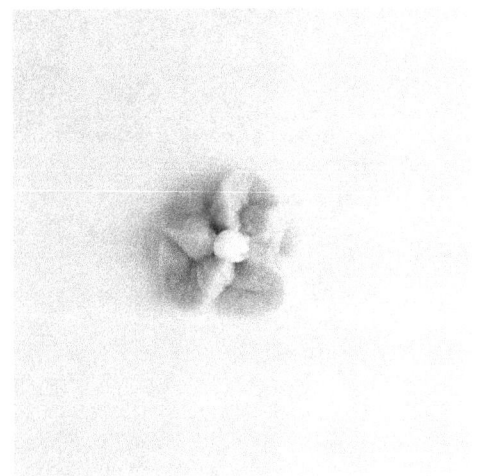

3 Releasing all pressure, lift the tip straight up and away to finish the flower. Pipe a dot in the center or add a small sugar pearl for a finished flower.

Piping Rosettes

Tip #17

Position: 90-degree angle from the surface of the cake

Medium-consistency frosting

1 Start by holding the piping bag straight up, slightly above the surface of the cake, and begin piping a star.

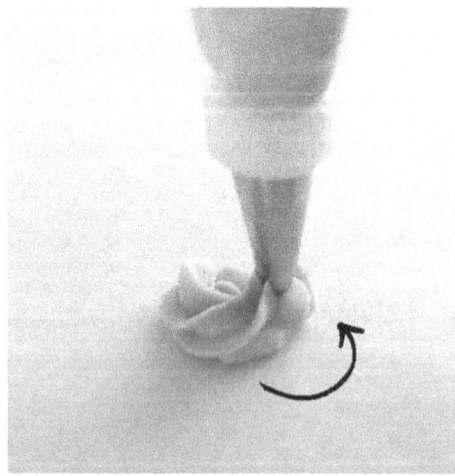

2 Maintaining steady, medium pressure, continue squeezing the bag, moving around the center star but keeping a tight design.

3 Continue piping until the outside ring is complete.

4 Releasing all pressure, lift the tip up and away to finish the rosette.

Piping Ruffles

Tip #104

Position: 45-degree angle from the surface of the cake

Thinner-consistency frosting

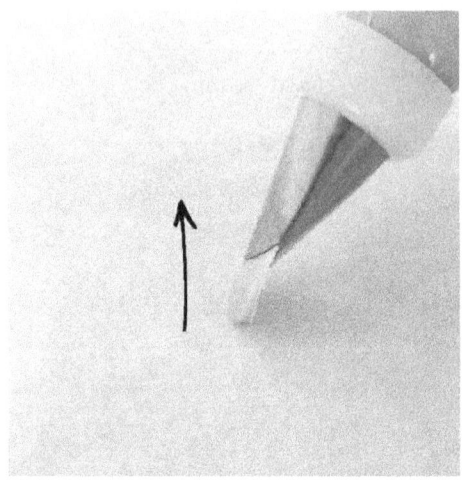

1 Position the wider side of the tip so that it is barely touching the surface. Begin squeezing with light to medium pressure, tilting your wrist to pull it up.

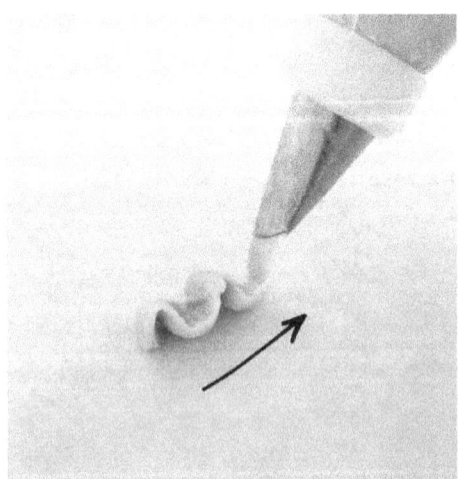

2 Then tilt your wrist down to create a ruffle.

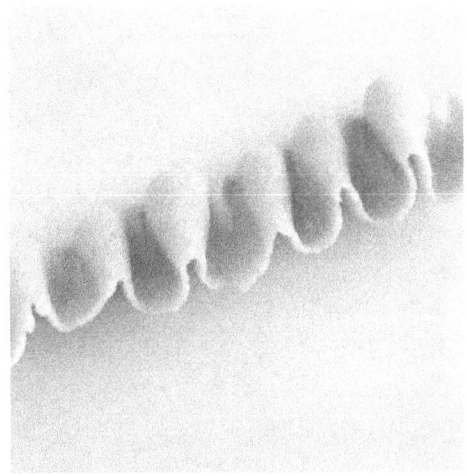

3 Repeat these up-and-down motions moving around the cake until you have a complete ruffle. These ruffles can be stacked to cover the entire surface of a cake.

Piping Leaves

Tip #67

Position: 45-degree angle from the surface of the cake

Thinner-consistency frosting

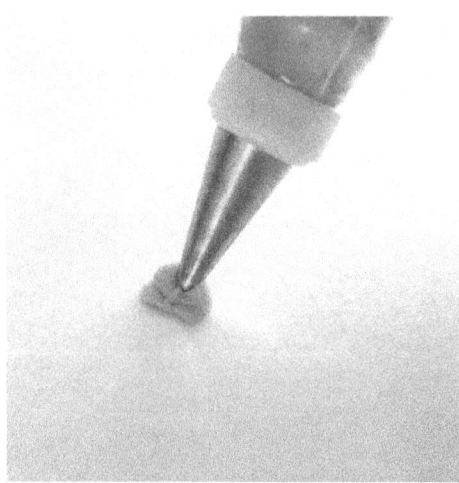

1 With medium pressure, squeeze the bag until a thick base of a leaf is formed.

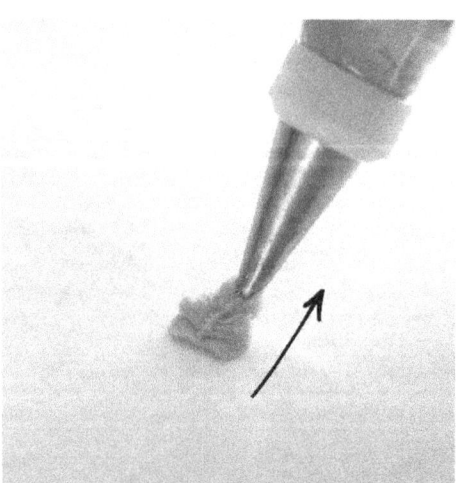

2 Continuing to squeeze, begin releasing pressure while pulling the tip away from the base so that the leaf narrows.

3 Releasing the pressure, pull the tip away quickly to get a point and finish the leaf.

Piping Grass/Hair

Tip #233

Position: 90-degree angle from the surface of the cake Slightly thinner-consistency frosting

1 Hold the piping bag straight up, slightly above the surface of the cake, and squeeze the bag with moderate pressure to form a base of frosting.

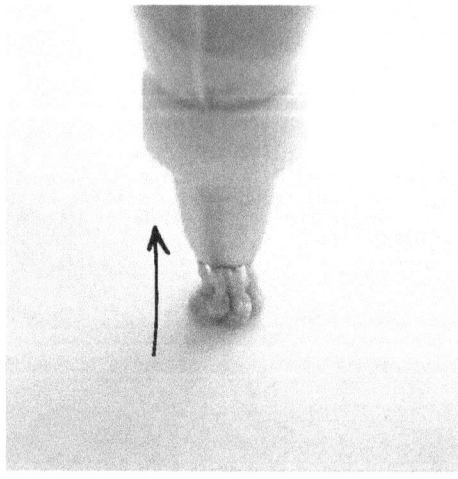

2 Releasing the pressure, begin lifting the tip straight up and away from the cake to finish. You can also pull up and to one side while releasing pressure to give it variations in direction.

3 Repeat to create your patch of grass or hair.

Going Big

Using a large piping tip to cover a cake in single or multiple large piped rosettes, stars, or dots is very popular right now. You might also use the same upsized piped decorations to create a wreath on a cake or a crescent-moon shape of designs around part of the top edge.

Using this decorating method, a single element like a rosette can be used, or multiple shapes can be mixed for a beautiful "bouquet" cake. The same supersize flowers, dots, or stars can be used on cupcakes for stunning designs. Rosette cupcakes are extremely popular and easy to execute in large quantities very quickly.

1 Using a large open-star tip such as #1M or #826 with medium-consistency frosting, begin in the center of the cupcake by holding the tip just above the surface at a 90-degree angle and piping a star with moderate pressure. Begin

lifting and slightly release the pressure, but do not pull away.

2 Continue squeezing the bag, moving around the center star with a tight design and keep spiraling until the rosette is complete.

WRITING AND PIPING SCROLLWORK

Writing on cakes is not my strongest gift and it took me ages to feel more confident about doing it. But with lots of practice, I've finally learned some important lessons that I hope will help you so that you don't struggle as much as I did.

Small round tips are the best for piping letters and lines on cakes. The sizes vary from extremely tiny to very large. For beginner cakes like those in this book, such as 8-inch round or 9-by-13-inch sheet cakes, a #3 or #4 round tip is a great size to start with. Cursive is difficult to master for most beginner decorators, so practicing different print fonts is a great place to start.

Scrollwork, decorative curls, swirls, and other patterns are all types of line work that are completed in a similar way as writing words or letters. Thin frosting is the best consistency for these techniques, and it's usually easier to pipe onto a chilled cake so that if you bump the surface, it won't be easily damaged. In an ideal situation, you will hold your piping tip just above the surface of the frosting and never actually touch it.

While you're still learning, it's best to practice first on parchment paper before piping directly on the cake. This will give you an idea of how large you need to make your letters andwhat style of letter you want to do. Practicing will also help you troubleshoot any problems you have before you're working on the cake. However, if you do make a mistake on the cake, you can use a toothpick to lift the letters off and try again. This is why it's important not to press into the frosting, but rather lightlypipe onto it.

Writing on Cake Tops

1. At the beginning of the letter, lightly touch the tip to the surface of the cake to anchor it.

Then, with steady, light pressure, hold your bag at a 45-degree angle barely above the surface of the frosting and begin piping your letters slowly, letting the stringof frosting drop to the cake in the desired lines or curves.

2. To break from one letter to the next, stop squeezing, touch the frosting tip lightly to the cake, and pull away. Clean any excess frosting from your tip before beginning another letter.

For writing in cursive or doing scrollwork, the same techniques will apply except you will not break between letters. Instead, you will use a continuous smooth motion, anchoring the frosting (touching the piping tip to the cake so that the frosting adheres) when you change directions so that the piped frosting doesn't pull away.

Four Tips for Better Freehand Designs on Cake

1. Measure the area where you will be writing, then practice on the same size paper or area. This way you'll know that your text will fit and be appropriately sized for your cake.

2. Lay a paper towel on the surface of your cake and use the straight edge as a guide so that your words stay straight and don't slant up or down.

3. If you're not confident with your freehand lettering, there are stamps available that

you can use to make an impression on crusted frosting before piping. Or for a simpler solution, use a toothpick to trace out the letters or "dot" them out before you start.
4. Sometimes spikes or tails will be present at the ends of your letters or lines. After the frosting crusts, use a damp finger to gently pat them down for a smooth finish.

Putting It Together

With all the piping techniques you've learned so far, you're now ready to put them together for beautiful texture effects and fun designs. Many of the basic piping skills can be slightly altered and used in patterns.

One of the most common elements with piping is using repetition to create borders on the bottom, and possibly also the top, edges of your cake. Another common decorating effect created by repetition is filling in an outlined shape with stars or dots to create a beautiful dramatic texture.

Piping Bead or Shell Borders

Tip #3 (bead) or #199 (border)

Position: 45-degree angle from the surface of the cake

Medium-consistency frosting

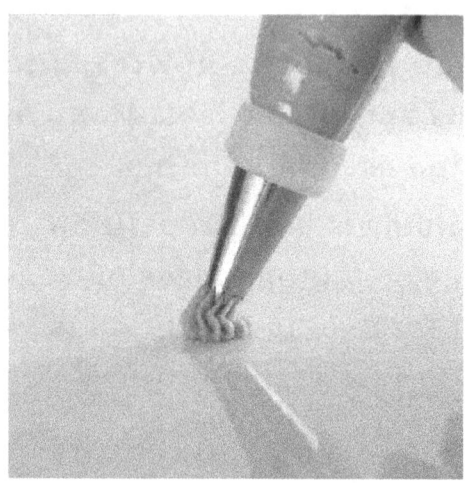

1 Hold the piping bag slightly above the surface of the cake. Squeeze until the frosting fans out and forms a foundation for your shape.

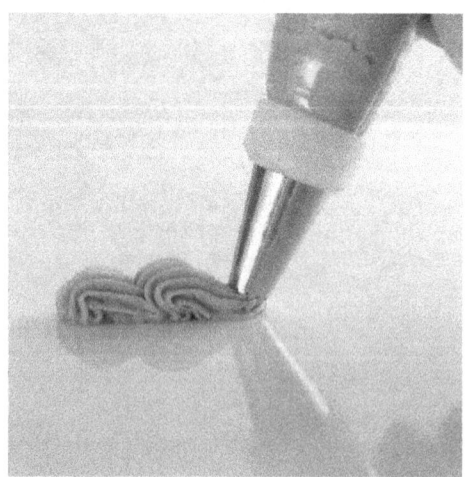

2 Without lifting the tip, move it toward you, slightly pulling it through the foundation, down toward the surface. Quickly release pressure until you reach the surface and the frosting breaks away.

3 Start the next shape directly on top of the pointed end of the previous one and repeat this pattern to form the border.

Filling In

Tip #17

Position: 90-degree angle from the surface of the cake

Medium-consistency frosting

1 Start by holding the piping bag at a 90-degree angle slightly above the surface of the cake. Pipe a line of stars in a tight formation.

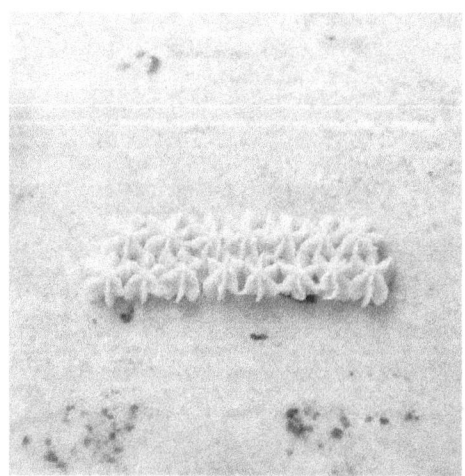

2 Starting very close to the first row, pipe a second row of stars close enough so that there are no empty spots between them.

3 Continue filling in until the space is completely covered. Touch up any areas that have blank spots.

COMBINING SHAPES

You can create beautiful cake designs by combining several of the piping techniques you just learned. Here's a quick example of combining a rosette with leaves and turning a star into a flower by adding a center dot. This could be the beginning of a design on a cake or would be perfect for the top of a cupcake.

Making Flowers Two Ways

1 Pipe a rosette, then add a leaf.

2 For balance, add another leaf on the other side.

3 Add some basic stars around the outside of the rosette.

4 Pipe dots into the center of the stars to turn them into sweet little flowers.

INSTRUCTIONAL CAKE

WREATH CAKE

Nothing brings more joy than beautiful flowers, and this WreathCake is just full of joy. Depending on the colors and flowers chosen, this cake can be bold, bright, and fun, or it can be soft, muted, and elegant. It's perfect for a birthday, Easter, or a romantic occasion.

TECHNIQUES USED:

Filling and Stacking a Cake Crumb-Coating a Cake Smooth-Frosting a Cake Adding Color to Buttercream Piping Grass
Piping Stars Piping RosettesPiping Leaves
Piping Swirl Flowers Writing on Cake Tops

YOU'LL NEED:

3 (8-inch) cake layers, stacked, filled, smooth-frosted with 5 cups Vanilla American Buttercream, and chilled
3 cups Vanilla American Buttercream, for decorating, dividedLight pink gel coloring
Regal purple gel coloringForest green gel coloringFinished
cake board Turntable
Piping bags with couplers Piping tips: #17, #18, #67, #233
White sugar pearls for flower centers and accents

1 Divide the decorating buttercream between 4 bowls. To the first, add a small drop of pink coloring; to the second a small drop of purple; to the third a tiny drop of green. Mix each until the color is fully incorporated. Leave the last bowl uncolored.

2 Place the chilled, crumb-coated cake on a finished cake board, then place it on a turntable.

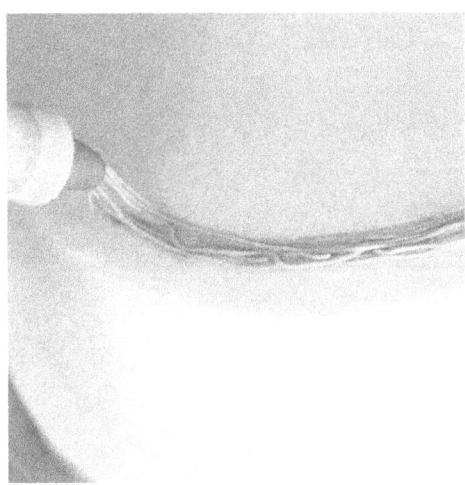

3 With a piping bag fitted with a #233 grass tip, approximately ½ inch from the outside edge of the top of the cake, pipe strands of green frosting in a "C" shape around two thirds of the cake.

4 With a piping bag fitted with a #17 star tip and filled with the white frosting, pipe small stars on the undecorated curve of the cake, leaving space between them to pipe rosettes.

5 With a piping bag fitted with the #18 tip, pipe small purple rosettes between the stars.

6 With a piping bag fitted with the #67 tip, add green leaves for accents.

7 With a piping bag fitted with the #18 tip, fill in some blank spaces with pink swirl flowers.

8 Add tiny white sugar pearls to the center of each flower.

9 Scatter more sugar pearls on the cake and pipe more leaves and tiny, white starflowers on the green part of the wreath.

10 Finish by filling in all the blank spaces with stars and swirl flowers, rounding out the arch of flowers on the wreath.

11 Add a name or message if you're celebrating a birthday or other occasion.

INSTRUCTIONAL CAKE

ELEGANT CHOCOLATE SHEET CAKE

Sheet cakes are sometimes considered out of style, but with theright decor, a sheet cake can be beautiful. When I see dark, monotone cakes like this, I feel like they're more masculine: perfect for a groom's cake or a guy's graduation cake. What's soawesome about this sheet cake is it's done with minimal tools. All of the flowers, stars, and borders are piped with a single tip.

TECHNIQUES USED:

Crumb-Coating a Cake Smooth-Frosting a Cake Piping Bead or Shell BordersPiping Stars
Piping Rosettes

YOU'LL NEED:

1 (9-by-13-inch) sheet cake, leveled, smooth-frosted with 3 cups Chocolate AmericanButtercream, and chilled
Finished cake board
Turntable
Piping bag
Piping tips: #1M, #4 round (optional, for lettering)
3 cups Chocolate American Buttercream, for decorating

1 Place the chilled, crumb-coated cake on a finished cake board.

2 Place a #1M piping tip (or similar tip) into a piping bag. Because this is a large tip, no coupler is needed. Snip off about 1 inch from the end of the bag, place the tip in the bag, then gradually trim the bag until about half the tip is exposed. Fill with the buttercream.

3 Starting at a corner, begin piping a shell-style border around the entire bottom edge of the cake.

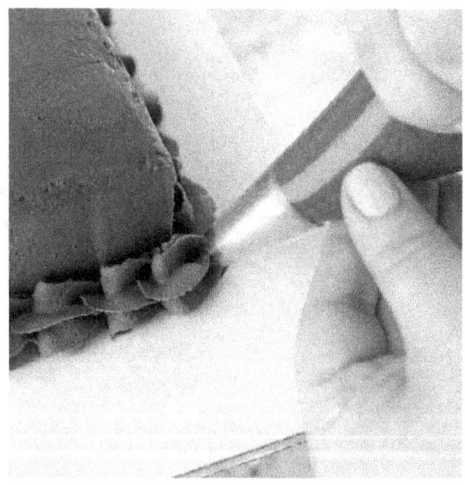

4 Keep piping until you get back to the starting corner.

5 Use a toothpick to mark off areas in opposite corners of the top of the cake to cover with piping. Having guides in place will help you know how much you want to cover.

6 Pipe three or four large and medium rosettes into the marked corner sections, filling most of the space.

7 Staying within or very near the guide marks, fill in the spaces with large stars or flowers.

INSTRUCTIONAL CAKE
A LITTLE LLAMA CAKE

From Mama Llama baby shower themes to video game characters and birthday parties, llama-themed parties and cakes are everywhere! They're so cute and fun, and you can simply change the colors and flavors to make this cake perfectfor any event.

TECHNIQUES USED:

Covering a Cake Board

Cutting Pieces from a Sheet Cake for a Figural CakeCrumb-Coating a Cake

Smooth-Frosting a Cake Adding Color to ButtercreamFilling In

Piping Ruffes

YOU'LL NEED:

1 (9-by-13-inch) sheet cake, chilled 9 cups Vanilla American Buttercream, for frostingand decorating 1 (14-by-19-inch) cake boardRed foil wrap

Cake template (here)Large serrated knife Small offset spatula

Piping bags, with couplers when applicable

Piping tips: large round #808, standard round #10, large multi-hole tip (grass tip), #104 ribbon tip Red gel food coloring

Sky blue gel food coloringYellow gel food coloring Black gel food coloring

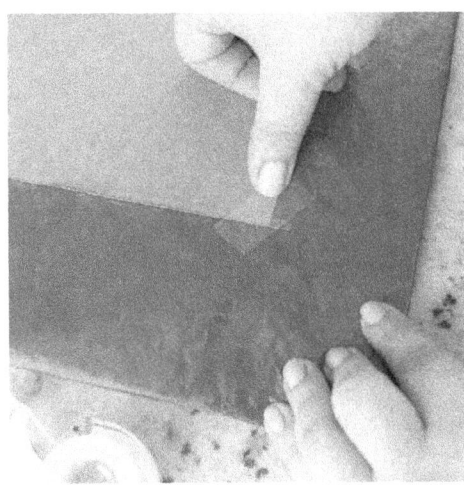

1 Cover the cake board with foil wrap to match the cake.

2 Using the template, cut the cake with a large serrated knife into the sections needed to make the llama. If you chill your cake before carving, there will be fewer crumbs and less chance of it tearing.

3 Arrange pieces on the the cake board in the shape of the llama: body in the center, legs on the bottom, head/neck on the top left with the ear on top, and then the tail.

4 Use a small offset spatula to crumb-coat just the top surface of the cake. It will not matter if this frosting has crumbs it in, because it will all be covered with more frosting.

5 For the sides of the cake, use a large round piping tip to pipe on frosting. Because many of the sides are soft, interior edges (from carving), piping is less likely to tear the cake. Also, the sides will not be decorated, so piping adds a thick layer of frosting that will not allow cake to show through.

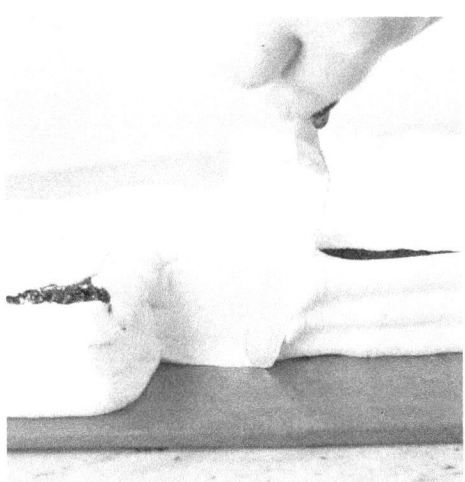

6 Using the small offset spatula, gently smooth the frosting on the sides, being careful not to touch the cake. Wipe off excess frosting as it accumulates on the spatula.

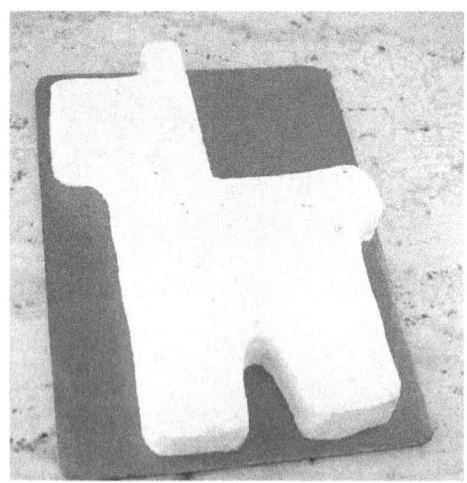

7 With the small spatula, smooth any top edges that need it and use a paper towel to get a final smooth finish (see here).

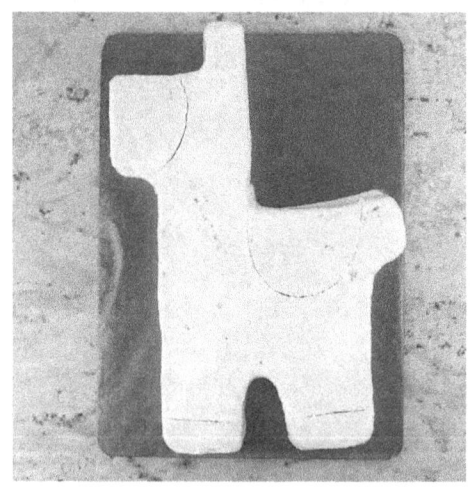

8 Use a toothpick to draw the lines for the face, saddle, and hooves.

9 Add some extra frosting and smooth it on the face of the llama. This is the only area on the top surface of the cake that will not be decorated, so you want to smooth-frost it and cover all crumbs.

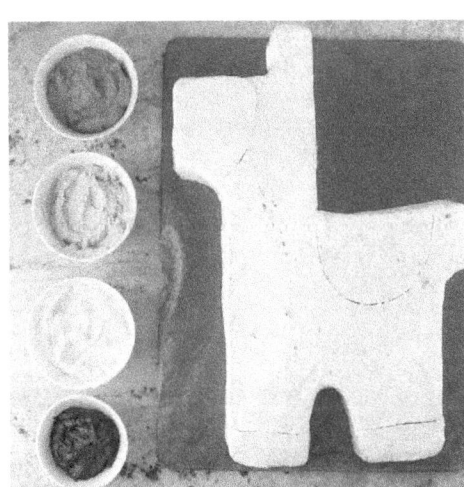

10 In each of 3 bowls place 1 cup buttercream and place ½ cup buttercream in a fourth. Color the ½ cup buttercream with 5 drops black gel coloring. Color the others with 5 drops red; 3 drops yellow; and 2 drops sky blue.

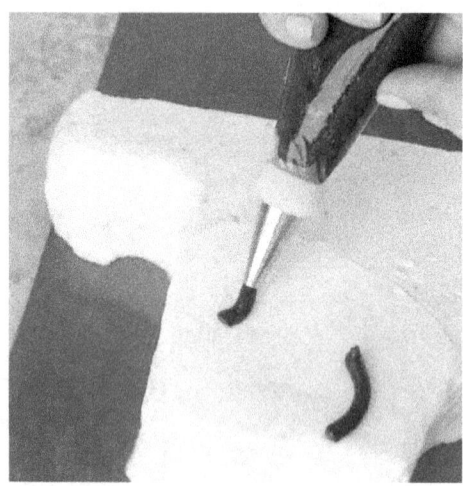

11 Using the #10 tip, pipe small black curves for the mouth and eyes; outline the contour of the llama's face.

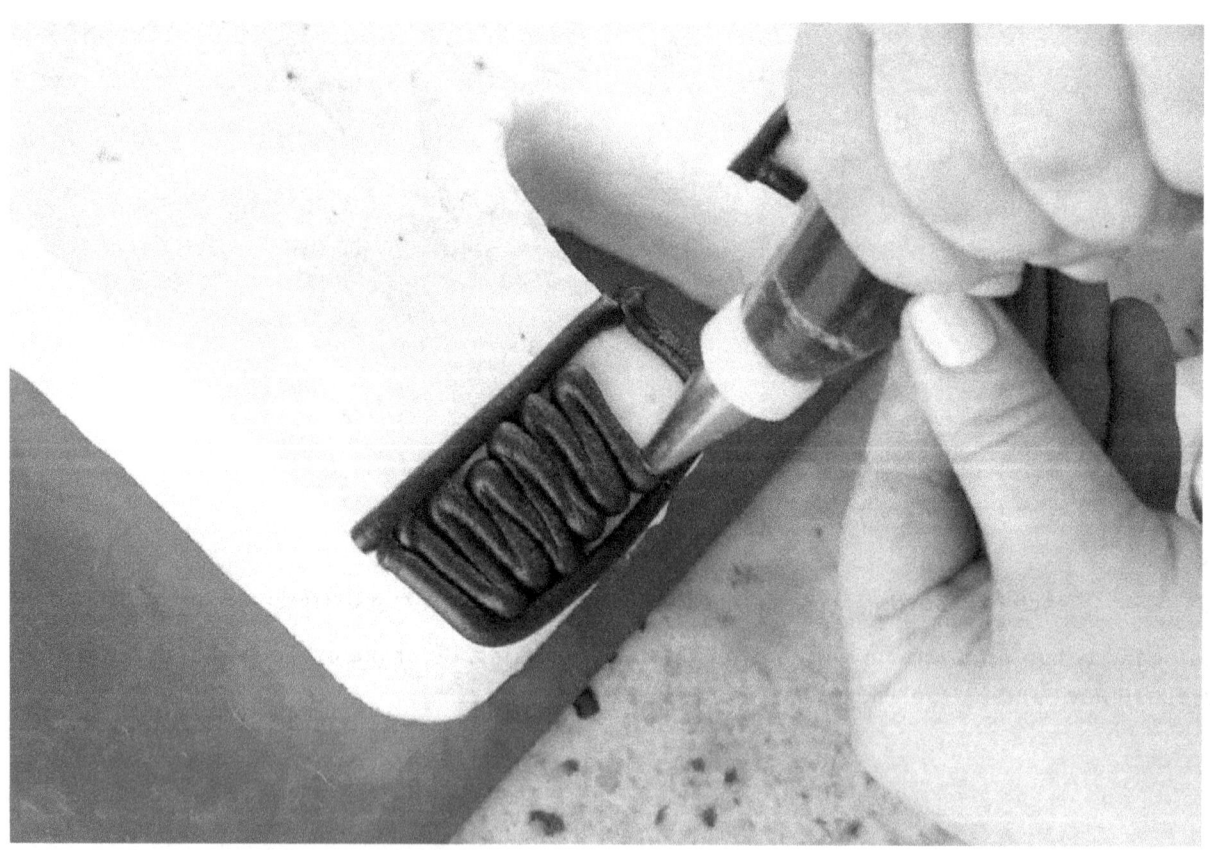

12 Continuing with the black frosting, pipe a rectangle on the bottom of each leg for hooves. Then, using a zigzag motion, fill in the hooves.

13 Using the multi-hole tip, pipe white "fur." These tufts of frosting don't have to be the same height; variation will give the cake beautiful texture.

14 Spread a small amount of yellow frosting at the top center of the saddle area using the small offset spatula.

15 Fit three piping bags with couplers and fill them halfway with red, blue, and yellow buttercream. You'll be piping ruffles with a #104 tip, so if you don't have three of the same tip, wash it between colors and alternate it among the three bags.

16 Begin piping ruffles on the outside of the saddle in a "U" shape. Alternate colors until you've filled the area and reached the yellow center area. Depending on the thickness of your ruffles, you will repeat the colors two or three times.

17 Pipe black a border on the inside of the ruffles to finish the saddle.

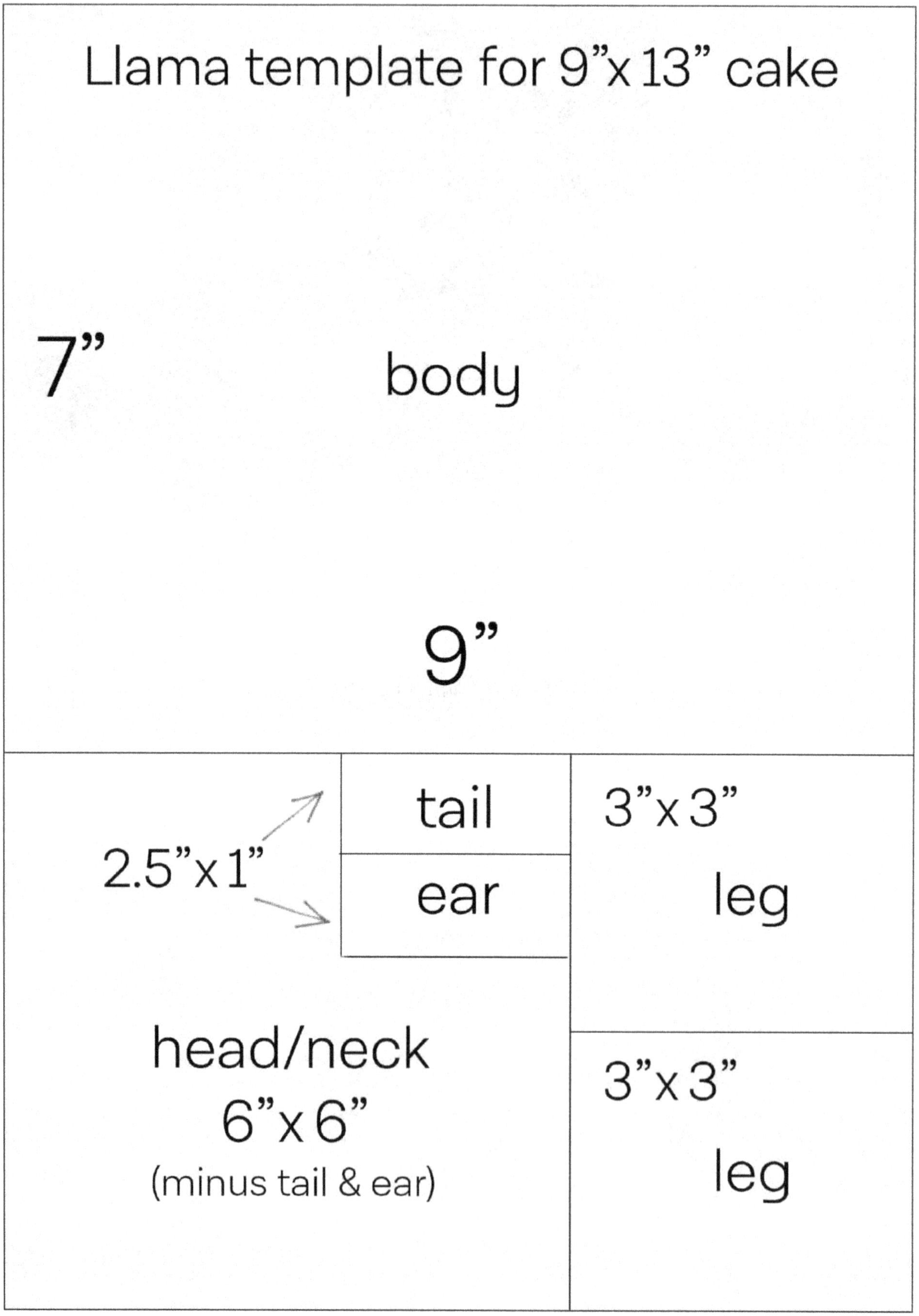

Llama template for 9"x 13" cake

7"

body

9"

2.5"x 1"

tail

ear

3"x 3" leg

head/neck
6"x 6"
(minus tail & ear)

3"x 3" leg

CHAPTER FIVE

Fondant Basics

When you're ready to move beyond buttercream, fondant is another medium for cake decorating that opens up a world of possibilities. There are a couple of different kinds of fondant, but when decorating cakes, the term "fondant" usually refers to rolled fondant.

Rolled fondant is a stretchy, flexible, doughlike sugar paste that can be cut into shapes, sculpted into figures, or rolled out and draped over cakes for a flawless finish. It's sweet and edible and brings your cake decorating to a higher level when mastered.

Buying or Making Fondant

Fondant is extremely popular for cake decorating and is readily available in most big-box stores, craft stores, and online, as well as in some grocery stores. It comes premade in a variety of colors, flavors, and brands. Fondant is more expensive than frosting, but it is well worth the price for the decorating possibilities.

If you prefer, you can make your own. My first big cake order, the one that prompted me to start a business, was my brother's wedding cake and his bride-to-be wanted her cake to be covered in fondant. Because some store-bought brands have a reputation for not tasting great and because I was on a budget, I decided to try my hand at making my own fondant. I've tweaked the recipe over the years, but homemade marshmallow fondant is my go-to fondant for almost all applications.

Homemade Marshmallow Fondant

YIELD: 3 POUNDS, ENOUGH TO COVER A 2-TIERED CAKE (6-INCH AND 8-INCH TIERS)

PREP TIME: 10 MINUTES, PLUS 2 HOURS OF REST TIME

This is so easy to make, and it tastes great, too. Made with mini marshmallows and a handful of other basic ingredients, it's extremely affordable and terrific for cake-decorating applications.

16 ounces mini marshmallows
¼ cup water, plus more for kneading
2 teaspoons vanilla extract or other liquid flavorsGel coloring (optional)
2 pounds (approximately 8 cups) powdered sugar, sifted
½ cup vegetable shortening

1. Pour the marshmallows into a large microwave-safe bowl. Pour the water over the top and microwave for 1 minute. Stirwith a silicone spatula, then microwave for another minute and stir again. If the marshmallows still are not completely melted and smooth, continue to microwave in 30-second increments and stir until you have a completely melted, smooth mixture.

2. Stir in the vanilla. If you need a whole batch of colored fondant, add gel coloring. Gently stir until well combined. Ifyou will not need the entire 3 pounds colored, see the "Adding Color to Fondant" technique.

3. Add the sugar and stir it into the melted marshmallows with the silicone spatula. It will not be easy, but continue stirring to incorporate as much as you can.

4. Use a small amount of the shortening to coat your hands andbegin to knead the dough in the bowl, continuing to incorporate the sugar until it comes together into a ball. If your mixture is crumbly or dry, add 1 tablespoon of water at atime and continue kneading until it comes together. (Note:

Your marshmallow mixture should have cooled enough to handle it at this point, but if you suspect that the mixture is still hot, wait a few minutes for it to cool. I like to work with it warm, but not so much so that I get burned.)

5. Coat your work surface with a thin layer of shortening, then dump the ball of fondant onto the surface and continue kneading until it's completely smooth. This shouldn't take more than a minute or two.

6. Shape the fondant into a ball and coat the outside with a thin layer of shortening, then wrap it in two layers of plastic wrap. Let it rest and cool for at least 2 hours before using. Do not refrigerate! It can be made days or weeks ahead of time and stored wrapped in an airtight container in a cool, dark place. If it's too hard to knead when you're ready to use it, remove the plastic wrap and microwave for 10 seconds to soften it again. Knead until smooth and stretchy, and then it's ready for use.

Adding Color to Fondant

Fondant can be colored to almost any hue. Since you'll be kneading it with your hands and gel colors can stain, wear food-safe gloves.

1 Coat your hands and work surface with a thin layer of vegetable shortening. Knead the fondant into a soft ball and make a small impression on the top. Then add color to the impression.

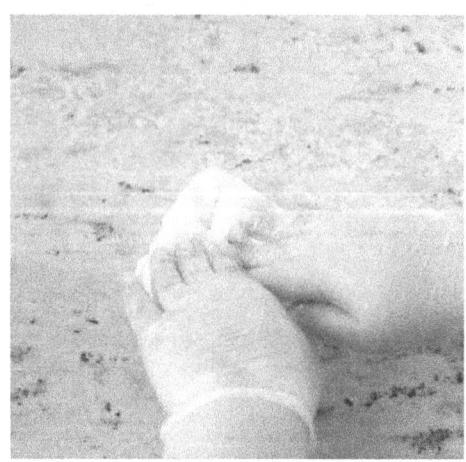

2 Fold the fondant over the color and begin to knead.

3 Continue to fold, stretch, and knead. If you stop at this stage and roll it out, it will look marbled.

4 Knead until there are no more streaks of color. Coat the fondant with a thin layer of shortening; wrap in plastic if not using immediately.

Working with Fondant

The most common use for fondant is covering a cake for a flawless finish. This can be done on a crumb-coated cake or a fully frosted cake, but whichever you choose, the surface under your fondant must be smooth. If there are any lumps or bumps under the fondant, it will be reflected in your fondant finish. I prefer a fully frosted and smoothed cake for this reason.

Any of the frosting recipes in this book will work under

fondant. Whichever frosting you choose, chill your frosted cake completely before covering in fondant. A cold cake is so much easier to work with.

Here are a few guidelines to make the process easier:

- Warm the fondant in a microwave in 10-second increments to soften it, carefully kneading it after each cook time to check for softness. Be careful: if microwaved too much, it can melt in the center and cause bad burns when you knead it! It is ready to use when it has the texture of smooth Play-Doh and the edges no longer crack when kneaded. Once it is soft enough, knead it into a smooth ball.

- For covering a cake or making decorative accents, roll out the fondant to approximately ⅛ inch thick, or 3mm to 4mm.

- To determine how large of a piece of fondant you'll need to rollout to cover your cake in one piece, measure how tall the cake is and how wide it is across the top. Then multiply the height by 2 and add the width. That will give you the minimum width to roll out your fondant.

- If air bubbles appear, you can use a very tiny pin to pop them and smooth them over.

APPROXIMATE AMOUNTS OF FONDANT NEEDED TO COVER 3-LAYER CAKES

	CAKE DIAMETER	WEIGHT OF FONDANT
Round Pans	6-inch	20 ounces
	8-inch	26 ounces
	10-inch	40 ounces
	12-inch	52 ounces
Square Pans	6-inch	26 ounces
	8-inch	40 ounces
	10-inch	52 ounces
	12-inch	78 ounces

Covering a Cake with Rolled Fondant

1. Dust the work surface with cornstarch or powdered sugar. Flatten the kneaded fondant a bit with your hand. Dust its surface, then set a rolling pin in the center and roll out toward the edges.

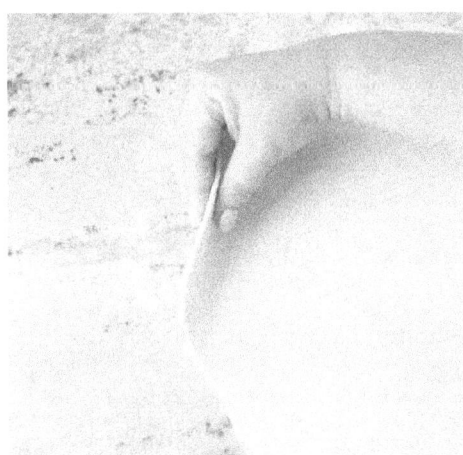

2. Continue rolling until the fondant is a uniform thickness ($\frac{1}{8}$ inch works best) and the size you need. Occasionally lift up the fondant and dust the work surface again so that the fondant does not stick.

3 Dust the surface of the fondant again. Place your rolling pin at the edge furthest from you. Roll the pin toward you, rolling the fondant onto it.

4 Lift the fondant up and unroll it onto your cold, crumb-coated cake set on a turntable.

5 Reposition the fondant so it's centered. Starting at the top of the cake, smooth the fondant so it adheres to the frosting. You can use your hands or a fondant smoother.
Work your way down, rotating the cake as needed until the fondant is completely smooth and adhered to the cake on all sides.

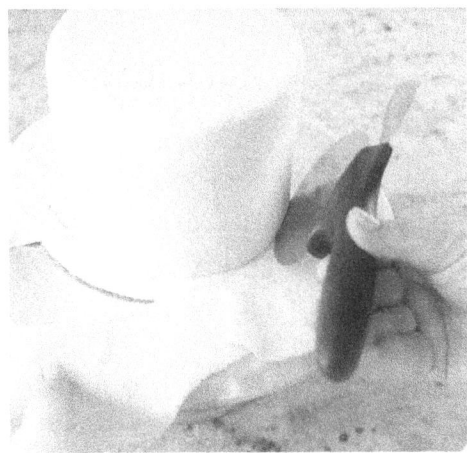

6 Use a pastry wheel, pizza cutter, or small paring knife to trim away the excess at the bottom edge.

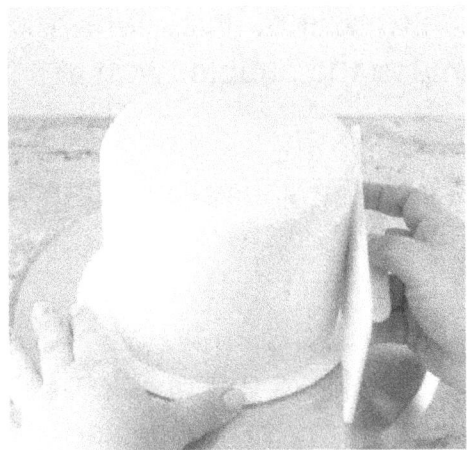

7 Use a smoother to smooth and polish the sides, pushing the fondant down to be even with the cake board if there are any gaps. Work any air bubbles down to the bottom edge, then smooth the fondant again.

COMMON MISTAKES WHEN WORKING WITH FONDANT

Fondant can be an intimidating medium for new cake

decorators, but it doesn't have to be. Here are some common problems and how to avoid or fix them.

- **The fondant is tearing.** You've rolled it too thin. When rolling fondant, do your best to keep your thickness uniform and at least ⅛ inch thick. The best thing to do is ball it up and reroll.

- **I can't lift the rolled fondant off the work surface.** If the fondant absorbs the cornstarch or powdered sugar, it will stick to your surface and tear when you try to move it. If it's just stuck a little bit, use a bench scraper to carefully detach it. If it's basically glued to the surface, it's best to scrape it up, ball it, and reroll, this time remembering to lift your fondant and dust the surface under it often as you roll.

- **My fondant looks cracked.** Don't leave fondant sitting out. It will dry out. This will lead to cracking or "elephant skin" when you drape it over a cake. Lightly coat it with shortening and keep it wrapped in plastic anytime you're not using it.

- **My fondant has air bubbles in it.** Knead your fondant until it's smooth but no further. Too much kneading can trap air bubbles, which will show up in your finished fondant. You can pop the bubbles with a small pin and smooth them over.

- **I don't have enough fondant to cover my cake.** If you roll out your fondant, place it on your cake, and begin smoothing only to find it's too short to cover the cake, you've either not used enough fondant or not rolled it thin enough. Always err on the side of generosity and use a little more than the charts recommend so that you don't have this problem. Since fondant is stretchy, sometimes you can continue smoothing and pushing until you've covered the gap. But if you truly are coming up short and don't want to start again, consider adding a ribbon border (such as the one used in the Sweet Flowers Wedding Cake recipe) or other fondant accent to cover the empty space.

USING FONDANT FOR DECORATIVE ACCENTS

One of the most popular uses of fondant is to cut out

decorations and accents, including dots, hearts, stars, flowers, bows, ribbons, ropes, and more. To get these shapes, you can use traditional cookie cutters, mini cookie cutters, special fondant cutters, or simply a small knife if you want to cut them by hand.

Fondant cutout decorations are easily attached to fondant-covered cakes with a tiny bit of shortening. Fondant decorations can also be attached to buttercream-covered cakes using water.

Making Rolled Fondant Accents with Cutters

1 Dust your work surface with powdered sugar or cornstarch. Roll out the fondant to ⅛ inch thickness.

2 Press the cutter into the fondant to cut out the shapes.

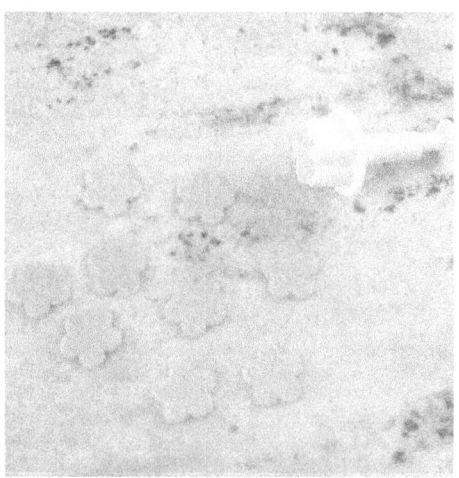

3 Detach the shapes from the sheet of fondant. Cover with plastic wrap or store in an airtight container, if you're not ready to use immediately.

INSTRUCTIONAL CAKE

SHADES OF BLUE HEXAGON CAKE

Requiring just a few simple techniques, this geometric design is sophisticated and modern.

TECHNIQUES USED:

Filling and Stacking a Cake
Crumb-Coating a Cake
Smooth-Frosting a Cake
Covering a Cake with Rolled Fondant
Adding Color to Fondant
Making Rolled Fondant Accents with Cutters

YOU'LL NEED:

8 ounces white fondant, for decoration
Navy blue gel coloring
Cornstarch or powdered sugar
Small rolling pin
Small hexagon cutter
Silver food spray
Food-safe gloves
Vegetable shortening
3 (8-inch) cake layers, stacked, filled, and frosted with 5 cups Vanilla American Buttercream, and covered in 26 ounces white fondant
Turntable

1. Divide the fondant for decoration into 3 equal balls. Keep one of them white. Add one drop of blue gel coloring to the second ball and two drops to the third ball. Knead the balls until the colors are uniform.

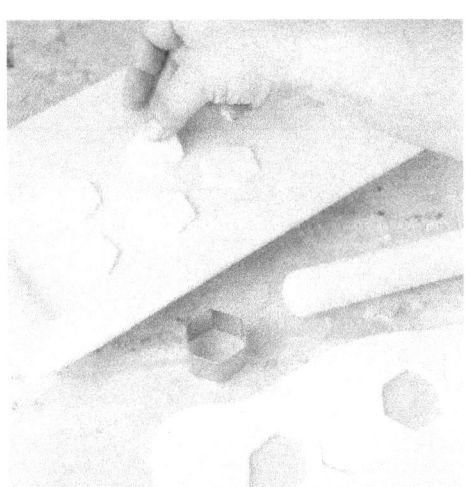

2. Dust the work surface with cornstarch or powdered sugar. Roll out the white fondant ⅛ inch thick with a small rolling pin. Cut out 12 hexagons with the cutter. Dust a platter or cookie sheet with cornstarch or powdered sugar, then place the hexagons on it. Ball up the extra white fondant, knead until smooth (warm in the microwave for 6 to 8 seconds, if needed), and roll it out again. Cut out another 12 to 16 hexagons. The number of hexagons needed for this design will vary depending on the size of your cutter and how you space and arrange the hexagons on the cake. You should have enough fondant to cut more if needed.

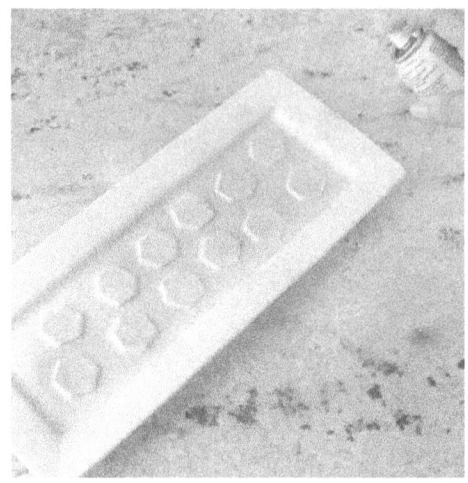

3 Spray half the white hexagons with the silver food spray. Set them aside to dry.

4 Roll out both balls of blue fondant. Cut out 12 to 16 hexagons from each.

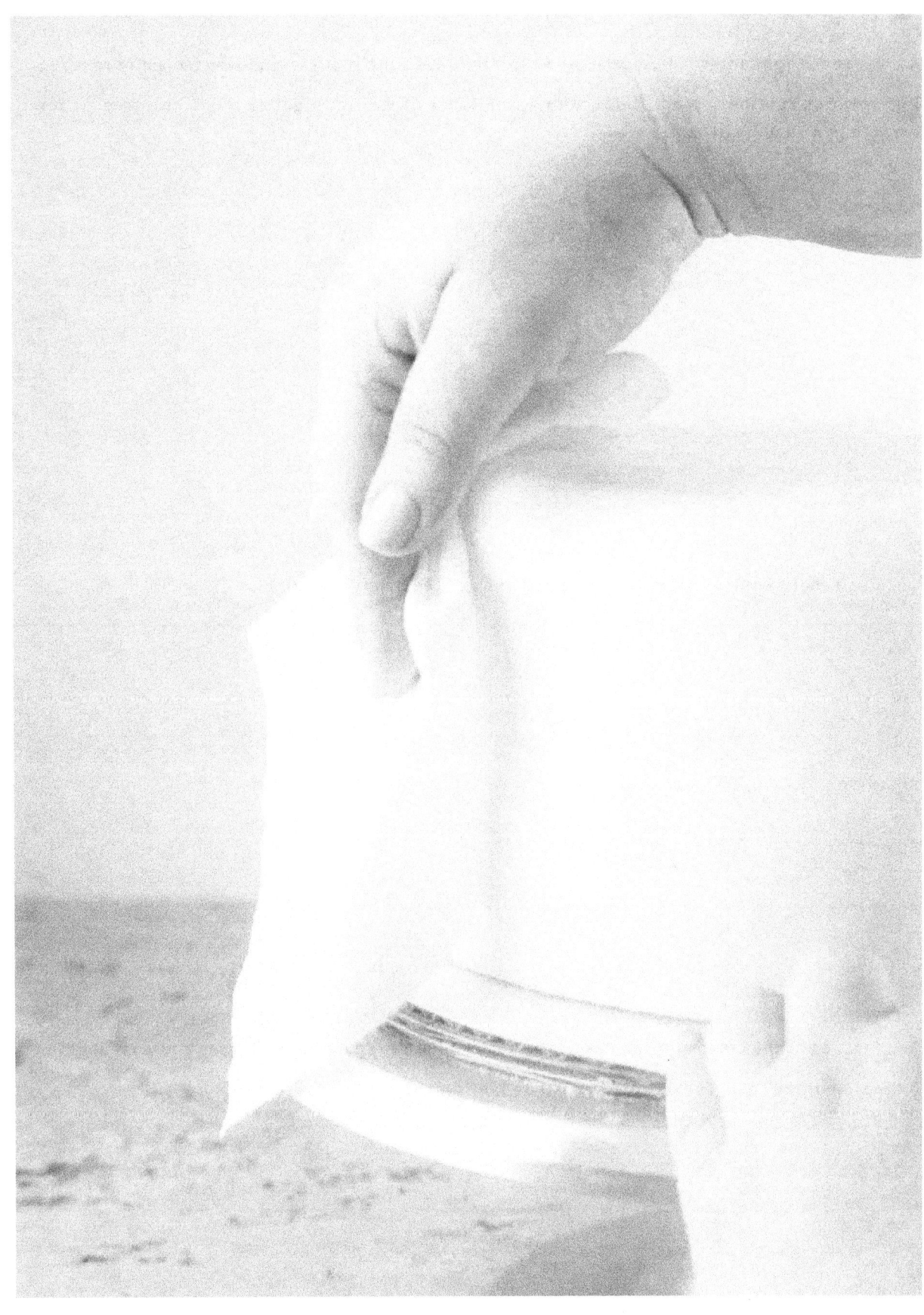

5 Place the fondant-covered cake on a turntable. Wearing food-safe gloves (so as not to leave fingerprints), rub the top and sides with a thin layer of shortening. Use a pattern-free paper towel to gently wipe off any excess.

6 Use a sharp knife or pastry wheel to cut some of the hexagons in half.

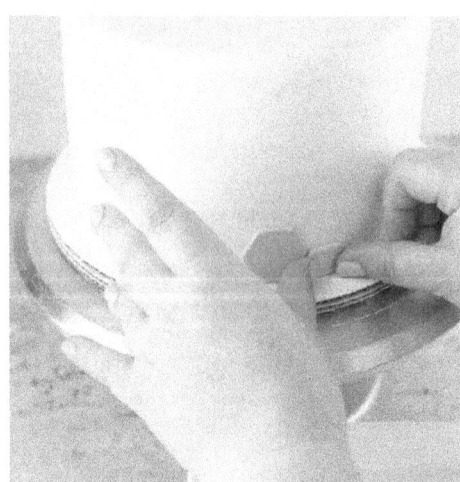

7 Starting at the bottom of the cake, attach dark blue hexagons, some halves and some whole, to the side of the cake. The pattern should be random.

8 Mix in some lighter blue and then white and silver hexagons as you work upwardand over the edge to the top of the cake. Keep adding them until you have a design that you're happy with.

INSTRUCTIONAL CAKE

SWEET FLOWERS WEDDING CAKE

This simple wedding cake can be the foundation for so many designs. In this tutorial, I will show you how to stack multiple tiers so that they are well supported and stable for transport. Iwill also share how to add fondant accents.

TECHNIQUES USED:

Filling and Stacking a CakeCrumb
-Coating a Cake Smooth-Frosting a
Cake
Covering a Cake with Rolled Fondant Making Rolled
Fondant Accents with Cutters

YOU'LL NEED:

3 (6-inch) cake layers and 3 (8-inch) cake layers, stacked in two tiers by size, filled, and frosted with 9 cups Vanilla American Buttercream, and covered in 46 ounceswhite fondant

Turntable

6-inch round cake pan6
bubble-tea straws Scissors

¼ cup buttercream or melted chocolate

12-inch wooden dowel rod, ¼-inch or ⅜ -inch thickMeat cleaver
or hammer

Cornstarch or powdered sugar

8 ounces white fondant for decoratingRibbon
cutter or ruler and pastry wheelRolling pin
Vegetable shorteningMini
flower cutter Small brush

Small white sugar pearls

1 Place the bottom 8-inch tier on a turntable. Place a clean 6-inch pan (which is the same size as the cake you'll be stacking there) centered on the top and lightly press down to leave a small mark.

2 Just inside the circle you marked, push a bubble-tea straw into the cake until it touches the bottom cake board. Mark the straw with a food-safe marker or small blade, so that when you cut it, it will be level with the fondant, then pull it out.

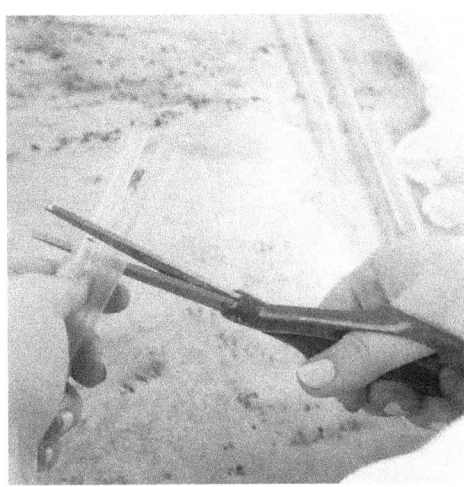

3 Cut all 6 straws at that length. The number of straws in a tier is equal to the diameter of the tier above it. This cake will have a 6-inch tier sitting on top of the 8-inch tier, so use 6 straws. Push them into the cake, evenly spaced, inside the circle.

4 Add the ¼ cup buttercream or melted chocolate to the center of the cake. This willhelp the top tier stay in place.

5 Take the 6-inch cake and center it on top of the 8-inch cake. When stacking multiple tiers, it's important that each tier has a cake board underneath it for support. Never stack multiple tiers without boards and proper support for each tier!

6 Sharpen a dowel rod with a pencil sharpener or knife, then measure it against the cake. Cut it to a length approximately ½ inch shy of the height of the cake.

7 Hold the dowel vertically in the center of the top tier, then hammer it into the cake.

When the dowel is nearly even with the top of the cake, line a small length of dowel up with it and gently tap on that until the first piece is below the surface of the cake. Fill the hole with a small ball of fondant or buttercream.

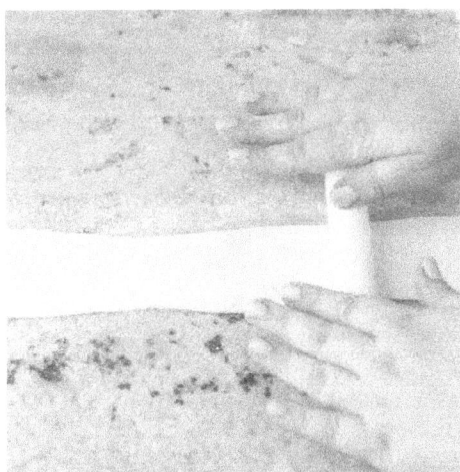

8 Dust your work surface with cornstarch or powdered sugar, then roll the fondant for decorating with the palms of your hands into a long rope. Use a rolling pin to roll

out the fondant lengthwise to ⅛ inch thickness.

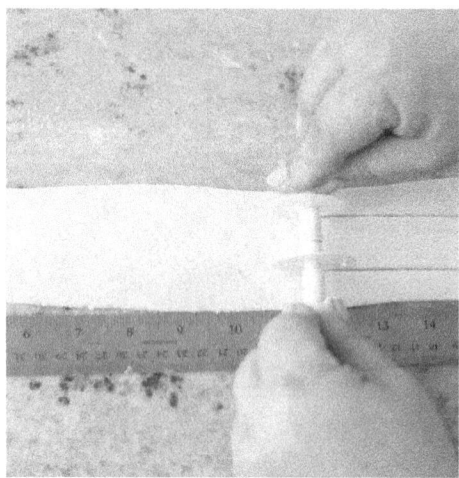

9 Use a ribbon cutter (or a ruler and pastry wheel) to cut a ribbon of fondant that is 1 inch wide. The length will need to be approximately 3 times longer than the size of the cake (an 8-inch cake needs a 24-inch ribbon, or slightly longer).

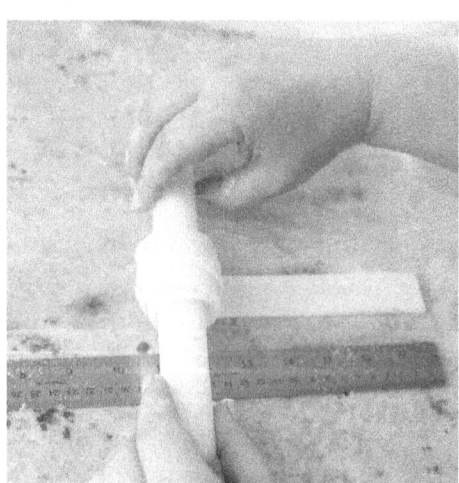

10 Dust the surface of the ribbon with cornstarch or powdered sugar, then roll it up onto a rolling pin.

11. Brush shortening around the base of each tier in a band approximately 1-inch wide.

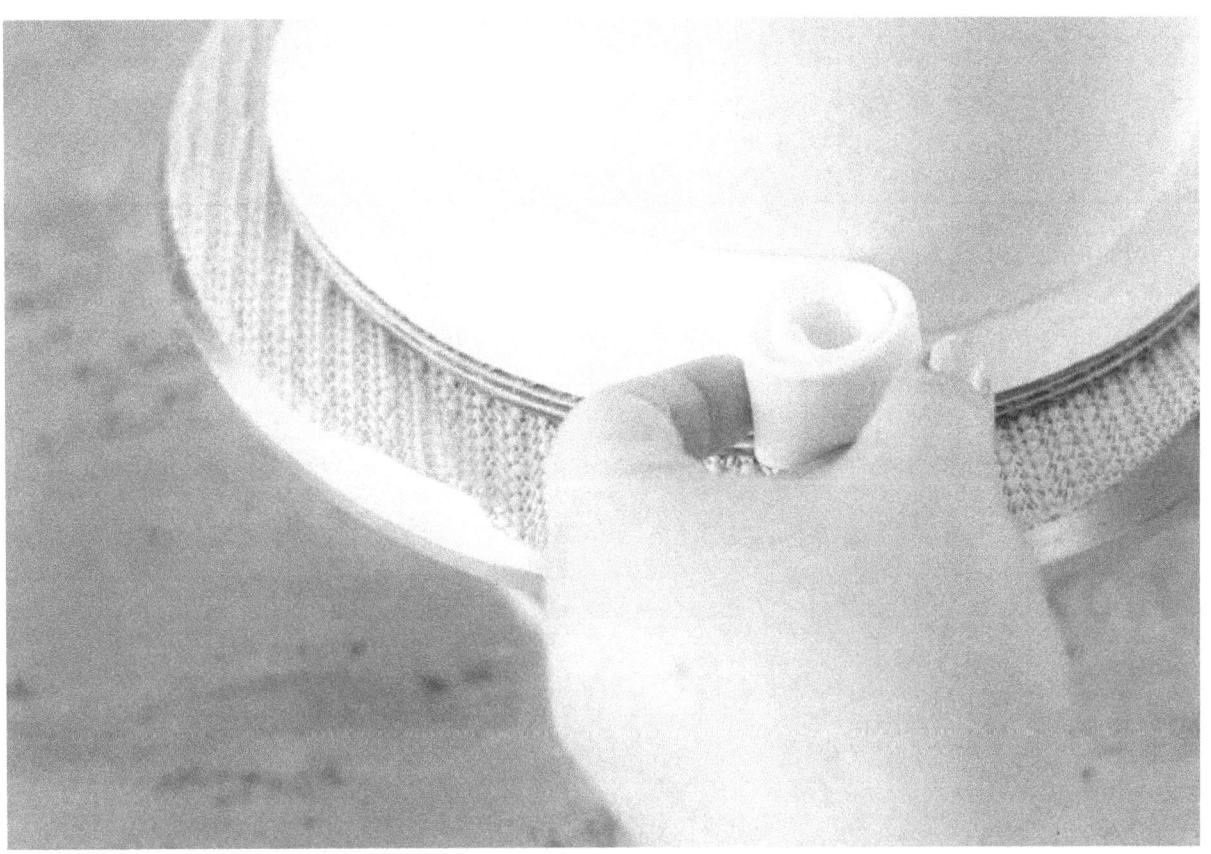

12. Slide the ribbon off the rolling pin. Starting at the back of the cake, unroll it as you move around the cake, adhering it to the bottom border. Cut off any excess at the back. Repeat the ribbon steps for both tiers.

13 Use a fondant smoother to smooth the ribbon and push it down in any places where it doesn't meet the board or the tier beneath it.

14 Place a quarter-size ball of fondant in a small bowl with a teaspoon of water. Melt it in a microwave to form sugar glue.

15 Roll out another ball of fondant to ⅛ inch thickness. Use a mini flower cutter to cut out flowers, then use the back end of a paintbrush handle to make a small hole in the center of each flower.

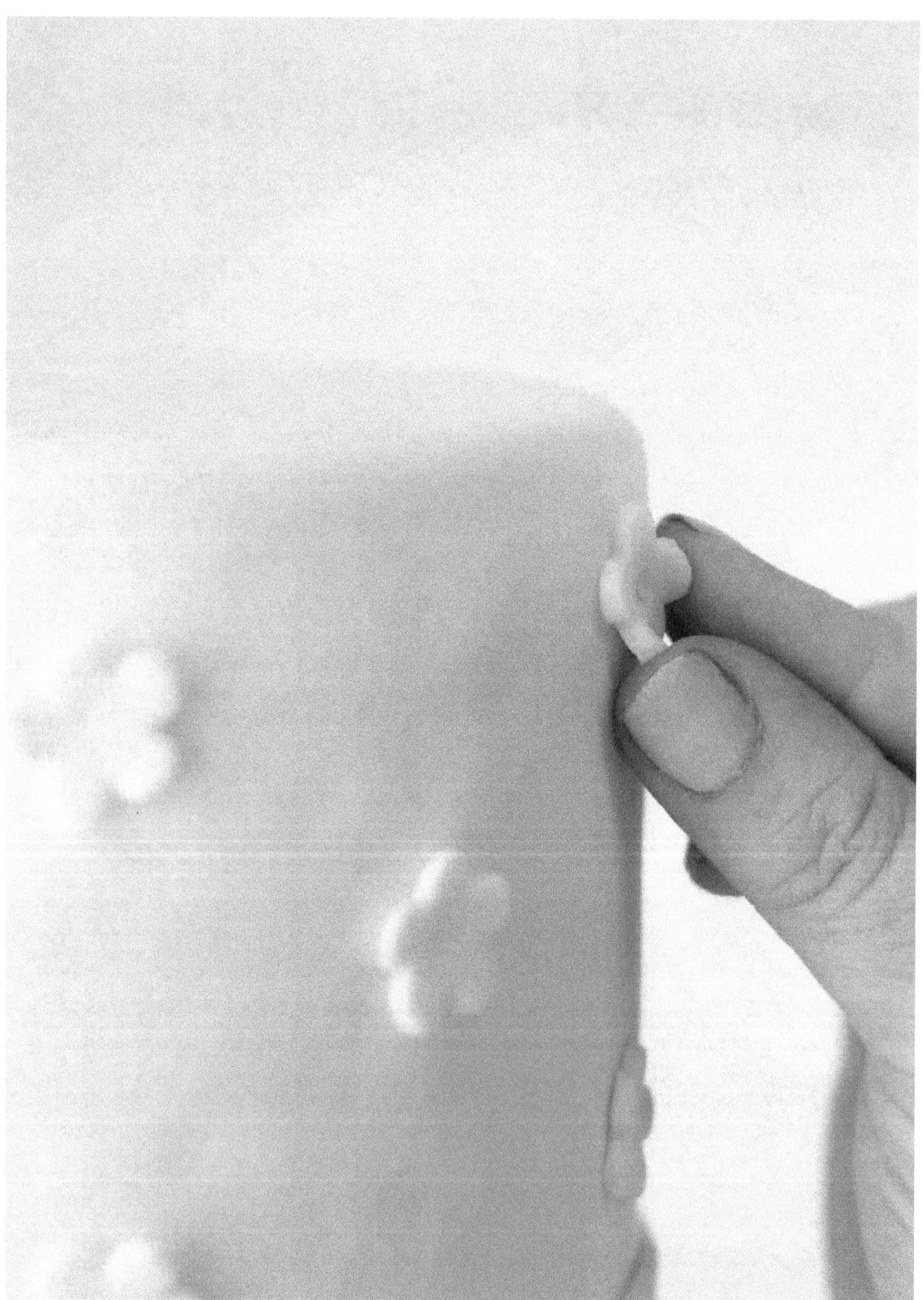

16 Use the sugar glue to attach the flowers to the top and sides of the cake in a regular pattern. Then paint a small dot of sugar glue in the center of each flower and add a sugar pearl.

CHAPTER SIX

Chocolate Basics

When I think of a timeless birthday cake, I think of a classic vanilla cake with chocolate buttercream. But that's never really been my style. For me, a *real* celebration has as much chocolate as possible. There's nothing more decadent than a chocolate cake with chocolate filling *and* chocolate frosting. It's rich, it's delicious, and it's what dreams are made of.

But if an all-chocolate dessert is too much (which seems impossible to me), you can still get your chocolate fix by using chocolate for decorations or as a complementary flavor to other ingredients, such as berries or caramel. With so many kinds of chocolate available, it's a versatile ingredient.

Types of Chocolate

When we think of chocolate, we're usually referring to the brown varieties: dark/bittersweet, semisweet, and milk chocolate. But there's also white chocolate. The benefit to white chocolate is not only a different yet amazing flavor, but also the ability to color it any shade of the rainbow for different cake designs.

Typically when decorating, you'll be using chocolate in the form of ganache.

Real White Chocolate vs. Candy Wafers

Candy wafers (Wilton markets them as Candy Melts™) are a common product used in the cake-decorating world and are often thought of as being "white chocolate." Also called almond bark, or powdered coating, candy wafers are not a bad product. In fact, they're easier to work with for many baking applications. However, it's important to note that they are not *real* white chocolate. White chocolate chips also behave differently than the other forms of candy wafers listed here. They include an ingredient to help them hold their shape when placed in baked goods, but that ingredient also makes it more difficult to melt them. I do not recommend white chocolate chips when making ganache.

Real white chocolate has cocoa butter as the fat ingredient, while the other products usually have palm oil as the fat. Real white chocolate is also not actually white, but slightly yellow in color from the cocoa butter and is notably more expensive than candy wafers.

I use candy wafers when I need colored "chocolate" for dripping because it's convenient, available in a variety of premade colors, and inexpensive. And for the inexperienced, it doesn't taste any different. However, for the best flavor, you'll want to buy quality white chocolate.

Chocolate Ganache

YIELD: 2 CUPS

PREP TIME: 5 MINUTES, PLUS COOLING TIME

Ganache is a rich mixture of chocolate and cream that can be used as a filling or frosting, as well as a glaze such as in the popular drip cakes. Ganache can be made with any kind of chocolate, but it's best with a darker, high-quality chocolate. I prefer to use semisweet chocolate that has a cacao content of 50 to 58 percent for the best flavor. Darker chocolate can be used, but the flavor will be very intense.

For this recipe, it's critical that you weigh your ingredients on a food scale rather than using measuring cups. The ratio of chocolate to cream is very important and weighed ingredients will be more accurate. You can use chocolate chips or you can buy your chocolate in bars or a brick; if you buy a bar or brick, chop it into small pieces before pouring the cream over it.

9 ounces heavy whipping cream
9 ounces semisweet or dark chocolate, chips or chopped

1. Pour the cream into a microwave-safe container and heat it in the microwave for 1 minute. Check it, then microwave again in 30-second increments until it's steamy. If you do not have a microwave, pour the cream into a medium saucepan and heat over medium heat until it begins to steam. Watch it closely, because you do not want to let it come to a full boil.

2. Put your chips or chopped chocolate in a heatproof measuring cup or bowl.

3. When the cream is heated, pour it over the chocolate, making sure the chocolate is covered, and let it sit for 1 to 2 minutes. Then gently stir it until it becomes smooth and shiny. If you have any chunks of chocolate that have not melted, return it to the microwave for 15 seconds, then stir again to

combine the chocolate and cream. Repeat as needed. If you're making ganache on the stovetop and you still have chunks, use the double-boiler method (place your heatproof bowl over a pot of simmering water) to heat the chocolate and continue stirring until smooth. Never place chocolate over direct heat.

4. For dripping, the ganache will need to cool for 10 to 15 minutes until it's slightly warm to the touch, or around 92°F if measured with a candy thermometer. For frosting or filling, allow it to cool completely or refrigerate for at least 30 minutes until it reaches a thicker, spreadable consistency. Then whip it on high speed with an electric hand mixer to get a fluffy, pipeable ganache.

VARIATION: WHITE CHOCOLATE GANACHE

Reduce the heavy cream to 3 ounces and substitute high-quality white chocolate for the semisweet or dark chocolate. This will yield about 1½ cups.

VARIATION: CANDY WAFER GLAZE

While it would not be a true ganache, if you want to make a ganache-like glaze with candy wafers that are pre-colored or bright white, use 12 ounces candy wafers, chopped, and 4 ounces heavy cream. This will yield about 2¼ cups.

Coloring White Chocolate

Coloring chocolate requires oil-based colors or "candy colors." You cannot use standard water-based colors in chocolate or it will seize, meaning it will become gritty and chunky. Chocolate is very sensitive to temperature, so do not add cold coloring to warm chocolate. It needs to be very close to the same temperature as the chocolate. You can warm the coloring by laying it on a heating pad or running warm water over the bottle or jar before using.

1 Pour the heated cream over the chocolate and stir until combined and smooth.

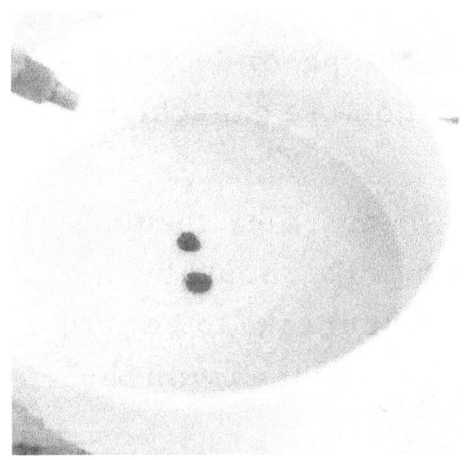

2 Add a drop or two of warm candy coloring to the ganache.

3 Gently stir until the color is fully mixed in. Stir in more if a darker color is desired.

Decorating with Ganache

Ganache can be used as glaze, dripping, frosting, filling, or decoration on cakes. One of the most important factors in how you use ganache is its temperature.

If you are using the ganache as a glaze or for a drip cake, the ideal temperature is 92°F. When using it as a glaze, the cake should be at room temperature. For drip cakes, you will want your cake to be very cold so that the ganache sets quickly when it makes contact with the cold surface and doesn't puddle at the bottom.

For filling and frosting cakes, the ganache needs to be cooler and thicker—close to room temperature with a texture similar to that of peanut butter. You can use it exactly like buttercream to fill a cake or cover a crumb-coated cake.

When it has completely cooled, ganache can also be whipped with an electric mixer on high speed into a light, fluffy frosting that can be piped like buttercream into beautiful borders or other designs.

Glazing a Cake with Ganache

Once the cake is covered, you can speed up the setting process by refrigerating it, but the ganache will become dull. Let it set at room temperature for about 3 hours if you want it to keep its glossy shine.

1 Set your crumb-coated cake on a wire rack set over a rimmed baking sheet. Begin pouring warm ganache in the center.

2 Continue pouring the ganache, moving outward to the sides and then pouring down the sides of the cake.

3 Spread the ganache on the side of the cake, smoothing any excess.

4 Let the cake stand until all dripping stops, then transfer to a cake board.

Using Ganache to Make Drips

Drippy cakes are all the rage and, with a little practice, you can master this easy, popular technique. Having the ganache in a squeeze bottle is my favorite way to do a drip cake, but you canalso use a spoon or a piping bag with the tip snipped off. If you have a candy thermometer, the ganache should be 92°F for theperfect drip, and the cake should be very cold. If you don't havea candy thermometer, your ganache should be barely warm to the touch.

Either way, you should always do a practice drip or two on the back of your cake to check how well it will drip before doingthe entire cake. If the ganache quickly runs to the bottom and pools, you will need to let it cool a little more or add more chocolate to thicken it. If it doesn't run at all or the drips are clumpy, you may need to warm it in the microwave for 5 to 10 seconds and stir again.

1 Place your chilled, crumb-coated cake on a finished cake board, then place it on a turntable. Have your warm ganache close by.

2 Hold your squeeze bottle (or piping bag or spoon) at a 45-degree angle just above the top edge of the cake and begin squeezing with the tip barely touching the cake (or dripping the ganache from the tip of the spoon).

3 Change the amount of ganache applied by adjusting the pressure you apply; alternate short and long drips for a natural look. Stop here if you only want the ganache as a drip on the sides. To cover the top as well, move on to steps 4 and 5.

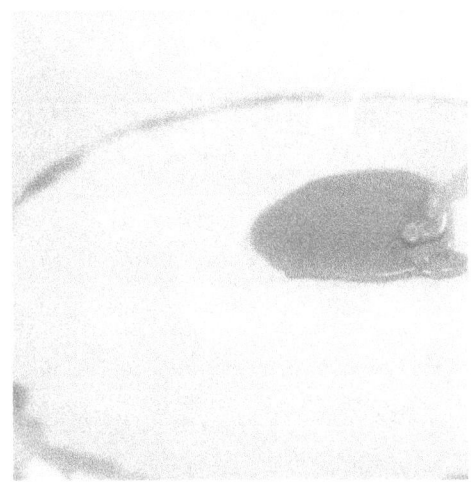

4 On the top of the cake, squeeze or spoon a puddle of ganache onto the center.

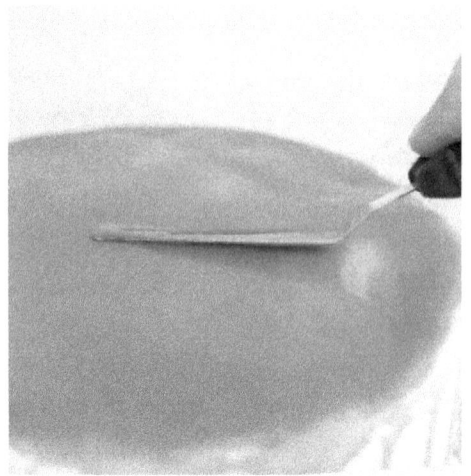

5 Spread and smooth the puddle, taking care not to push any extra over the edge. You want it to blend into the drips on the edge without overtaking them. Add more ganache in small amounts if needed.

6 Let the cake stand until the drips are set (about 5 minutes) before doing any other decorations.

INSTRUCTIONAL CAKE
SWEETHEART CHOCOLATE CAKE

The first time I had this cake and frosting combination, my bestfriend Kathy shared it with me. I've been hooked ever since. This lovely heart cake is perfect for a romantic dinner or small party, and no special pans are required. It's a triple threat of chocolate
—chocolate cake, chocolate ganache, and whipped-ganache frosting.

TECHNIQUES USED:

Adding Color to Buttercream

Cutting Pieces from a Sheet Cake for a Figural CakeFilling and Stacking a Cake

Crumb-Coating a Cake Glazing a Cake with GanachePiping Stars and Rosettes Piping Bead or Shell Borders

YOU'LL NEED:

3 cups Vanilla American Buttercream, dividedRed gel coloring

Heart template

1 (9-by-3-inch) chocolate sheet cake Sharp knife8- and 10-inch round cake boards Scissors Cooling rack

Large baking sheet

2 cups Chocolate Ganache, dividedSmall offset spatula

Cake lifter

Finished cake board

Large piping tips #822 and #825

Gold candies, star sprinkles, and edible pearlsElectric mixer

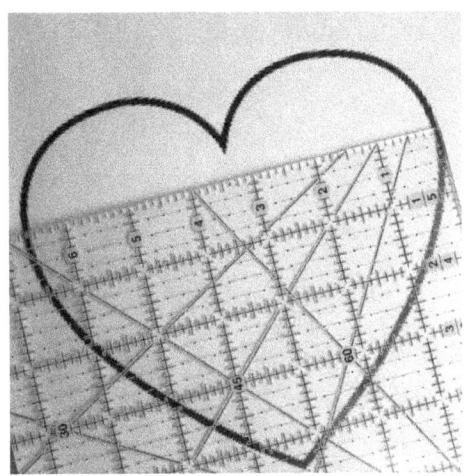

1 Color 1 cup of the buttercream red with approximately ¼ teaspoon of red gel coloring (see here for tips on rich colors) and let it develop while you prepare the cake. Create a heart template that is 6½ inches across at its widest point and 6 inches high.

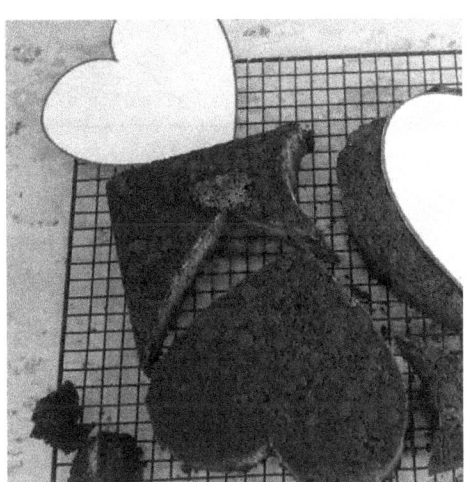

2 Print two copies of the heart template, place them on the sheet cake, and carve out two hearts with a sharp knife. Also, cut an 8-inch round cake board into the heartshape with the template.

3. Stack and fill the heart layers on the heart-shaped cake board with the uncolored buttercream. Set on a 10-inch cake board; crumb-coat and chill at least 20 minutes.

4. Place the cake on a rack over a baking sheet, then cover the cake with 1 cup of the slightly warm ganache and smooth it with an offset spatula to a glossy finish.
Allow it to set for at least 10 minutes.

5 Using a cake lifter and small spatula, carefully lift the ganache-covered cake and move it back to the cake board.

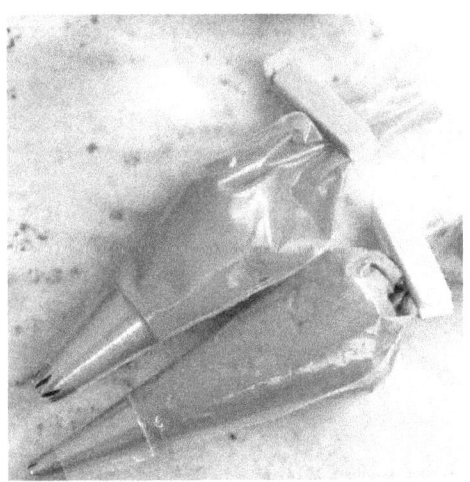

6 Chill the remaining ganache until firm, whip until fluffy, and put it in a piping bag fitted with a #822 large open star tip. Put the red frosting in a bag fitted with a #825 tip.

7 Starting on the outer edge and moving inward, pipe large stars, small stars, and small rosettes onto the top left section and along the board on the lower right side. Alternate the colors and shapes to achieve a balanced design.

8 Add gold candies, sprinkles, and sugar pearls. Then, pipe a border of ganache around the bottom edge of the cake.

INSTRUCTIONAL CAKE

BRIGHT & HAPPy SPRINKLES CAKE

Pink is my favorite color and this bright, happy cake brings all the smiles. While it will look like you worked on it all day, this cake comes together surprisingly fast and has a big "wow" effect. In addition to being my favorite color, this cake also joinscream cheese frosting with rich chocolate cake—an incredible, mouthwatering combination.

TECHNIQUES USED:

Filling and Stacking a CakeCrumb
-Coating a Cake Smooth-Frosting a
Cake
Adding Sprinkles to the Side of a Cake (see Heart & Sprinkles Cake)Adding Color to
Fondant
Making Rolled Fondant Accents with CuttersColoring White
Chocolate
Using Ganache to Make DripsPiping Stars

YOU'LL NEED:

3 (8-inch) chocolate cake layers, stacked, filled, crumb-coated, and smooth-frosted with 5 cups bright pink Crusting Cream Cheese Frosting

Turntable

Large baking sheet

1 cup (8 ounces) sprinkles mix (pink,turquoise,
purple, and white)
1 ounce white fondant, colored with3 drops
turquoise gel coloring
1 ounce white fondant, colored with3 drops
purple gel coloring

Small rolling pin

Small flower punch-cutter and mold

½ cup White Chocolate Ganache (here), for dripping, colored purple with

2 drops candy coloring
2 cups bright pink Crusting Cream Cheese Frosting, for decorating Large piping tip #867

1 Place the smooth-frosted cake on a turntable. Place the turntable on the baking sheet and press sprinkles along the bottom edge of the cake. You can easily pour the sprinkles that fall onto the baking sheet back into your jar to reuse them. After the sprinkles are attached to the side of the cake, chill it while you make the fondant flowers.

2 Roll out the purple and turquoise fondant ⅛ inch thick. With the small flower punch-cutter, cut out small flowers from each color and use the mold to shape them.

3 Add small flowers randomly to the sides of the cake.

4 Add a drip of purple ganache to the top edge of the cake. Put the cake in the refrigerator for 10 minutes.

5 Fill a large piping bag fitted with a #867 large tip with the pink cream cheese frosting. When the drip on the cake is set, pipe large swirls on top of the cake around the edge.

6 Add more sprinkles and fondant flowers to the top of the cake and the frosting swirls.

Common Mistakes Making Ganache

- Ganache is sensitive to temperature. If the cream is too hot or food coloring too cold, it will "seize," meaning you'll have a clumpy, grainy mess. Most seized ganache can be fixed by reheating it to 92°F and gently stirring until smooth. If that doesn't work, try adding a teaspoon of warm milk and stirring.

- If stirred too much or too aggressively, ganache can end up with a gritty texture. The fix for this is the same as for seized ganache.
- Brands of chocolate and heavy cream vary slightly in water content, fat content, etc. For this reason, you might end up with ganache that's too soft or too firm once it's set, even if you follow the measurements in the recipe exactly. When this happens, adjust the chocolate to cream ratio to get the desired consistency the next time: Add more chocolate if it's too soft; add less if your ganache is too firm.

Measurement Conversions

VOLUME EQUIVALENTS (LIQUID)

US STANDARD	US STANDARD (OUNCES)	METRIC (APPROXIMATE)
2 tablespoons	1 fl. oz.	30 mL
¼ cup	2 fl. oz.	60 mL
½ cup	4 fl. oz.	120 mL
1 cup	8 fl. oz.	240 mL
1½ cups	12 fl. oz.	355 mL
2 cups or 1 pint	16 fl. oz.	475 mL
4 cups or 1 quart	32 fl. oz.	1 L
1 gallon	128 fl. oz.	4 L

VOLUME EQUIVALENTS (DRY)

US STANDARD	METRIC (APPROXIMATE)
⅛ teaspoon	0.5 mL
¼ teaspoon	1 mL
½ teaspoon	2 mL
¾ teaspoon	4 mL
1 teaspoon	5 mL
1 tablespoon	15 mL
¼ cup	59 mL
⅓ cup	79 mL
½ cup	118 mL
⅔ cup	156 mL
¾ cup	177 mL
1 cup	235 mL
2 cups or 1 pint	475 mL
3 cups	700 mL
4 cups or 1 quart	1 L

OVEN TEMPERATURES

FAHRENHEIT	CELSIUS (APPROXIMATE)
250°F	120°C
300°F	150°C
325°F	165°C
350°F	180°C
375°F	190°C
400°F	200°C
425°F	220°C
450°F	230°C

WEIGHT EQUIVALENTS

US STANDARD	METRIC (APPROXIMATE)
½ ounce	15 g
1 ounce	30 g
2 ounces	60 g
4 ounces	115 g
8 ounces	225 g
12 ounces	340 g
16 ounces or 1 pound	455 g

Resources

CountryKitchenSA.com: This is where I buy most of my supplies—cookie cutters, gelcolors, cupcake liners, cake drums, tools, cake pans, and so much more.

FondantSource.com: This is a great resource for reasonably priced pre-colored fondant in a variety of brands.

Amazon.com: If I need a tool or ingredient quickly, I get it through Amazon Prime.

BRPBoxshop.com: This is the only place I order cake boards (rounds) and pretty, bakery-style boxes from.

WholesaleSugarFlowers.com: This is an incredible resource for premade sugar flowers.

Sweetapolita.com: I love the sprinkles selection here.

Hobby Lobby: This is where I can get premade toppers, some cake supplies, paper to cover my cake boards, and so on.

Michael's: This chain of craft stores has a good selection of cake-decorating supplies.

Walmart: This is where I get almost all my ingredients, and I can often find cake-decorating supplies in a pinch.

CPSIA information can be obtained
at www.ICGtesting.com
Printed in the USA
BVHW062246180521
607552BV00006B/1012